On Becoming
Exceptional

Also available from ASQ Quality Press:

A Lean Guide to Transforming Healthcare: How to Implement Lean Principles in Hospitals, Medical Offices, Clinics, and Other Healthcare Organizations
Thomas G. Zidel

The Internal Auditing Pocket Guide: Preparing, Performing, Reporting and Follow-up, Second Edition
J.P. Russell

Improving Healthcare Using Toyota Lean Production Methods: 46 Steps for Improvement, Second Edition
Robert Chalice

Insights to Performance Excellence 2007: An Inside Look at the 2007 Baldrige Award Criteria
Mark L. Blazey

Root Cause Analysis: Simplified Tools and Techniques, Second Edition
Bjørn Andersen and Tom Fagerhaug

The Certified Manager of Quality/Organizational Excellence Handbook, Third Edition
Russell T. Westcott, editor

IWA-1:2005 Quality management systems—Guidelines for process improvements in health service organizations
ISO

Making Change Work: Practical Tools for Overcoming Human Resistance to Change
Brien Palmer

Transactional Six Sigma for Green Belts: Maximizing Service and Manufacturing Processes
Samuel E. Windsor

5S for Service Organizations and Offices: A Lean Look at Improvements
Debashis Sarkar

Leadership For Results: Removing Barriers to Success for People, Projects, and Processes
Tom Barker

To request a complimentary catalog of ASQ Quality Press publications, call 800-248-1946, or visit our Web site at http://www.asq.org/quality-press.

On Becoming Exceptional

SSM Health Care's Journey to Baldrige and Beyond

Sister Mary Jean Ryan, FSM

ASQ Quality Press
Milwaukee, Wisconsin

American Society for Quality, Quality Press, Milwaukee 53203
© 2007 by American Society for Quality
All rights reserved. Published 2007
Printed in the United States of America
12 11 10 09 08 07 06   5 4 3 2 1

Library of Congress Cataloging-in-Publication Data

Ryan, Mary Jean, Sister, 1938–
    The challenge to be great : on becoming exceptional : SSM health care's journey to Baldrige and beyond / Sister Mary Jean Ryan.
        p. ; cm.
    ISBN 978-0-87389-715-0 (alk. paper)
    1. SSM Health Care (Saint Louis, Mo.)—History.   2. Baldrige National Quality Program (National Institute of Standards and Technology)   3. Hospitals—Missouri—Saint Louis—Awards.   4. Catholic health facilities—Missouri—Saint Louis—History.   I. Title.
    [DNLM: 1. SSM Health Care (Saint Louis, Mo.)   2. Baldrige National Quality Program (National Institute of Standards and Technology)   3. Awards and Prizes—Missouri.   4. Hospitals, Voluntary—organization & administration—Missouri.   5. Efficiency, Organizational—Missouri.   6. Total Quality Management—Missouri.   WX 159.5 R989c 2007]
    RA982.S2S77 2007
    362.1109778'66—dc22
                                                        2007006922

Publisher: William A. Tony
Acquisitions Editor: Matt Meinholz
Project Editor: Paul O'Mara
Production Administrator: Randall Benson

ASQ Mission: The American Society for Quality advances individual, organizational, and community excellence worldwide through learning, quality improvement, and knowledge exchange.

Attention Bookstores, Wholesalers, Schools, and Corporations: ASQ Quality Press books, videotapes, audiotapes, and software are available at quantity discounts with bulk purchases for business, educational, or instructional use. For information, please contact ASQ Quality Press at 800-248-1946, or write to ASQ Quality Press, P.O. Box 3005, Milwaukee, WI 53201-3005.

To place orders or to request a free copy of the ASQ Quality Press Publications Catalog, including ASQ membership information, call 800-248-1946. Visit our Web site at www.asq.org or http://qualitypress.asq.org.

Quality Press
600 N. Plankinton Avenue
Milwaukee, Wisconsin 53203
Call toll free 800-248-1946
Fax 414-272-1734
www.asq.org
http://www.asq.org/quality-press
http://standardsgroup.asq.org
E-mail: authors@asq.org

∞ Printed on acid-free paper

This book is dedicated to the employees, physicians, and volunteers of SSM Health Care, who every day in every way reveal the healing presence of God.

And to my congregation, the Franciscan Sisters of Mary, who have supported and encouraged me and provided opportunities I could never have dreamed of.

Contents

List of Figures . . . . *xi*

Foreword . . . . *xiii*

Preface . . . . *xv*

Acknowledgments . . . . *xvii*

Introduction . . . . *xix*

Chapter 1   **From Five Sisters with \$5**
            to Baldrige **1**
            Our Roots   3
            My Early Years in Health Care   7
            Some Stories   9
            Looking in the Mirror   10
            SSM Health Care   11
            Preservation of the Earth   13
            Nonviolent and Inclusive Language   14
            Prayer   15
            Diversity   15

Chapter 2   **A Conversation over a Beer** **19**
            Our Leadership Conferences   19
            Improving the Complex Processes of
                Health Care   22

	An Experience in the Operating Room	23
	Applying Manufacturing Principles to Health Care	24
	CQI: The Journey Begins	25

Chapter 3   **CQI: The First Tentative Steps** **27**

	A New Language	27
	Senior Leaders as Teachers	29
	A Change in Culture	30
	An Example from the Emergency Department	31
	Working in Teams	32
	Some Good Things	35
	Some Not-So-Good Things	35
	Resistance to Change	38
	CQI and Physicians	39
	Clinical Collaboratives	40
	Thinking Differently	42

Chapter 4   **The Baldrige Push** **45**

	State Quality Award Programs	46
	A Psychological Boost	46
	An Open Culture	48
	Our Dry-Run Baldrige Application	49
	Mind the Gaps	51
	How the Baldrige Application Works	52

Chapter 5   **Our Mission** **55**

	Articulating What Already Existed in People's Hearts	55
	The Mission Development Process	56
	Deep Conversation	57
	Getting to the Essence	59
	Presenting the Mission to the Board	59

	The Rollout	60
	Stories of Commitment and Healing	63

Chapter 6 **Applying for the Baldrige—Three Times, No Charm** **65**

The Nun and the Nice Jewish Guy 65
Our First Try 67
Back to the Drawing Board 70
If at First You Don't Succeed 72
The Feedback 74

Chapter 7 **Making the Connections** **77**

Passports 77
Knee Bones, Thigh Bones: It's All
    about Alignment. 78
Department Posters 78
Meeting in a Box 80
Revealing the Healing Presence of
    God. 82

Chapter 8 **Baldrige One More Time** **85**

The Call from the Secretary of
    Commerce 88
A Thank-You 88
A Story 89

Chapter 9 **The Ceremony** **93**

Chapter 10 **Learning from Baldrige** **95**

Three Key Messages 96
How Do You Know You're Good? 96
Opportunities for Improvement 96
Sharing Our Story 97
Framework, Focus, Discipline 99

Chapter 11 **Beyond Baldrige** **101**

Many Challenges 101

The Scandal of Our Broken Health
　　　　Care System 102

Leadership at All Levels 103

Owning the Work 104

SSM University 106

School at Work and VOICE 106

A Fair and Just Culture 108

Going Tobacco-Free................. 109

Healthy Living 111

Achieving Exceptional Patient Care 111

A Matter of Integrity 115

Chapter 12 **In Conclusion** **117**

Index *119*

List of Figures

Figure 1	Sister Mary Jean Ryan in 2006..	xx
Figure 2	Early photo of Mother Odilia and the sisters.	3
Figure 3	Mother Odilia.	4
Figure 4	Our Dear Lord's.	5
Figure 5	African-American Franciscan Sister of Mary with child.	6
Figure 6	Sister Mary Jean as a young nurse.	7
Figure 7	St. Mary's Hospital, Madison, Wisconsin.	8
Figure 8	Bill Thompson.	11
Figure 9	Steve Barney.	16
Figure 10	Yvonne Tisdel	16
Figure 11	Sister Mary Jean at the 1987 SSM leadership conference.	20
Figure 12	Sister Mary Jean as an operating room nursing supervisor.	24
Figure 13	Barb Funches teaches a CQI class at our Good Samaritan Regional Health Center in Mt. Vernon, Illinois..	29
Figure 14	Father Jim Krings.	31
Figure 15	SSM St. Joseph Hospital West.	32
Figure 16	Peter Vrabec.	33
Figure 17	SSM Health Care System Seven-Step CQI Model.. . .	36
Figure 18	Lynn Widmer.	38
Figure 19	Dr. Andy Kosseff.	40
Figure 20	Dr. Fil Ferrigni.	41
Figure 21	Sister Susan Scholl.	42
Figure 22	Mary Calcaterra.	43
Figure 23	St. Francis Hospital & Health Services, Maryville, Missouri.	47
Figure 24	Showcase for Sharing.	49

Figure 25   Ron Levy.   52
Figure 26   The lobby at SSM Health Care's corporate office
in St. Louis..   56
Figure 27   Suzy Farren..   58
Figure 28   Mission brochure.   62
Figure 29   "Nun and nice Jewish guy" ad.   66
Figure 30   Passports..   69
Figure 31   Laura Jelle, the "queen of quality."   73
Figure 32   A department poster.   79
Figure 33   Meeting in a Box   80
Figure 34   Tom Langston..   82
Figure 35   SSM Cardinal Glennon Children's Medical Center. . .   83
Figure 36   Paula Friedman..   86
Figure 37   Bill Schoenhard.   87
Figure 38   One of our Baldrige applications.   89
Figure 39   "Great things come from great people" ad..   90
Figure 40   Sister Mary Jean accepts the Baldrige Award from
Vice President Dick Cheney..   94
Figure 41   Doug Ries..   97
Figure 42   An SSM University School at Work 2006 graduating
class.   107
Figure 43   Materials for the Achieving Exceptional Patient
Care Meeting in a Box..   112
Figure 44   Sherry Hausmann..   114

Foreword

This book tells the honest story of an organization—SSM Health Care—and a person—Sister Mary Jean Ryan— who dared to dream about what health care could be and then had the vision, determination, guts, and stamina to pursue that dream. It is the story of the hard work, disappointment, and joy that accompany the commitment to excel.

The book combines (1) the description of a multi-year and multi-tear journey that should inspire all organizations to take the improvement challenge with (2) the personal stories of Sister Mary Jean, a caring person and superb storyteller.

My own role in the story began with a conversation I had with Sister Mary Jean over lunch at a meeting we were both attending in 2001. She challenged me about whether the Baldrige bar was set too high and could not be achieved in health care. It was a frank and painful lunch. I don't think I ate much; I certainly didn't enjoy what I was being fed by the waiter or Sister! But I believe we both left that lunch with renewed inspiration. For Sister Mary Jean, I believe there was a renewed commitment to delivering exceptional health services. For me, there was a renewed commitment to the power of the Baldrige Criteria to drive organizations to systematic improvement and innovation. Sister Mary Jean had challenged me to make sure we delivered on our responsibility to guide organizations to achieve "the leading edge of validated management practice," not only in business but in health care and education. In this book she will entertain you and challenge you and your organization as well.

Too often today, leaders and organizations focus only on the short-term, accepting long-term benefits only if they can be derived from short-term efforts. Visionary leaders know how to balance short-term and long-term goals. They always question the status quo. They always celebrate current victories while establishing long-term goals. Visionary leaders are the single most common characteristic among Baldrige Award recipients. Baldrige is about people, processes, and results. Choosing two out of three will not lead to sustainable organizations or leaders. This book shows the power of visionary leaders and organizations that focus on all three.

Sister Mary Jean has helped me appreciate that those of us who work for and volunteer our time to the Baldrige program do it to make a difference for our country. Sister Mary Jean and SSM Health Care show how they have made a difference in the delivery of health care and the caring with which it is delivered. But most importantly, their story should show you, the reader, how you can and why you should strive to excel in your organization. I encourage you to take the challenge!

Harry Hertz
Director, Baldrige National Quality Program

Preface

My purpose in writing this book is to share SSM Health Care's story and to let others know that it has taken incredible persistence to move a large and complex health system out of its complacency with being better than average. My message to you is this: Hang in there. It's hard work. But it is possible to transform an organization.

For us, the answer was continuous quality improvement (CQI) and the Malcolm Baldrige National Quality Award process. CQI gave us a culture that relished improvement, and Baldrige gave us the focus we needed. Without doubt, the high point on our journey was being the first health care organization to receive the Baldrige Award, in 2002. But the award was by no means the end of the story, because we are more determined than ever to improve. And we still have so far to go.

Acknowledgments

This book could not have been written without the women and men of SSM Health Care, because they are the ones who, day in and day out, live our mission. In the years since we formed SSM Health Care as a system, we have changed considerably. In the beginning, we were a loose configuration of hospitals and other health care facilities; our only commonality was the fact that we were founded by our sisters. Today we are an organization that constantly shares, grows, and looks for ways to do things better. Today we are an organization that is becoming exceptional.

Many people have helped us along the way. Certainly Dr. Don Berwick and Maureen Bisognano and others at the Institute for Healthcare Improvement have provided invaluable support and immeasurable inspiration. They have been vocal proponents of safer, better health care in this nation. They truly are heroes of the twenty-first century.

I would like to thank Bobbi Linkemer for her research and editorial assistance in preparing this book, Paul Wagman for his help with the stories, and Suzy Farren for her invaluable assistance throughout the project.

Introduction

If you are considering buying this book, please heed this warning. It does not deliver five or ten magical steps to levitate your organization to excellence. Instead, it tells a story of mundane realities—hard work, dozens of mistakes, and the extraordinary commitment of thousands of people. It deals with blind alleys, unpopular decisions, incremental improvements, and even a few breakthroughs. In other words, it deals with the real world of flawed organizations and human beings. So if your taste in the business-management aisle of the bookstore runs toward fantasy, please keep looking. If, on the other hand, you are interested in learning from someone who will readily admit her—and her organization's—myriad faults, multiple mistakes, and constant doubts . . . well, then, it is my ardent hope that there is some bit of wisdom here that will help you.

But first, a story.

In 1985, I was on a small plane—eight seats—on my way back to St. Louis from St. Eugene Hospital in Dillon, South Carolina, where another senior executive and a consultant had spent the day explaining our new structure to the hospital's administrative team. As the plane took off, we congratulated ourselves on the success of the meeting. We were forming a new structure, a health system—SSM Health Care—that would give our hospitals greater control over their day-to-day management. Hospital administration was pleased that they would no longer have to submit routine requests to a board, a process they rightly considered micromanagement.

Suddenly, the plane began to dip and bump. My first thought was that it would smooth out after a few seconds, but it didn't. The turbulence persisted for several minutes. Finally, it seemed that there was only one thing to do. And that's the only time in my life I ever drank Scotch. (Actually, I'm a beer person.)

I tell this story to illustrate a couple of points. First, even though I'm a Catholic nun, I'm a pragmatic woman. And second, I recognize that sometimes you have to do what it takes to get through the bumpy ride. At SSM Health Care, our ride has never been smooth. There have been times of great optimism, when we felt we had discovered the answer, only to be faced with incredible turbulence. But we have endured—and for the most part without Scotch.

This book, then, is an attempt to tell the story of SSM and how we made our way through the turbulence. If you are seeking some wisdom from this book, let me summarize what I have come to understand. For us, there has been only one path: the path that would move us closer to our mission of exceptional health care services. Even though there were bumps along the way, we never deviated from the path. So the kernel of wisdom is this: Hold on to your vision even in the darkest, most turbulent days.

Figure 1   Sister Mary Jean Ryan in 2006.

1

From Five Sisters with $5 to Baldrige

Until 2002, when we became the first health care organization to receive the Malcolm Baldrige National Quality Award—given by the president of the United States for outstanding achievement in quality—few people outside the health care community had ever heard of SSM Health Care. We were a Catholic health system in the Midwest—certainly not the largest, or the richest, by any measure. Nor were we seeking those distinctions. Our goal for several years had been to be the *best* at providing exceptional health care to our patients. But outside our organization, few even knew that. For the most part we labored in obscurity, despite a history that stretched back more than a century, to 1872.

That was when five courageous Catholic sisters arrived in St. Louis with five dollars to their name. They had come from Germany, where Catholics were being persecuted, and they spoke no English. But they were determined to meet the health needs of their times, and to do that, they wanted to start a religious congregation. During their first winter in St. Louis, they were referred to as the Smallpox Sisters because of their devoted care to people stricken with that deadly and contagious disease (fortunately, the name didn't stick).

Such a beginning. So much to be inspired by; so much to live up to. In the early twenty-first century, as CEO of SSM

1

Health Care, I feel morally obligated to meet the needs of people in today's world.

The Baldrige Award came as a tribute to the inspiration offered by those sisters, and, of course, to everyone at SSM today—some 34,000 employees, physicians, and volunteers in all. The award demonstrated that a health care organization could achieve exceptional results. It showed that SSM Health Care could indeed chart its own course in a turbulent and constantly changing health care environment.

Charting our own course has become part of our organizational character. When others in health care hired consultants to guide their efforts, we often chose to figure things out for ourselves. As a result, over the years, we've done a lot of making things up as we go along. When we couldn't find templates to follow, we created our own—when we created a new culture through continuous quality improvement; when we ratcheted up our efforts to meet the Baldrige Criteria, the toughest and most respected in American business; and, most recently, when we created our own approach to improving the satisfaction of our patients and their loved ones.

> *Remaining true to our mission is the glue that holds us together, the end-all and be-all, if you will—our reason for being.*

Along the way, we've generated a lot of interest, not only from the health care community, but from business organizations all over the world. They want to know how we took a slightly better than average health care organization that had been around for more than a century and revitalized it so that better than average was no longer acceptable. They want to know how, after we galvanized our more than 24,000 employees, we actually managed to translate their support into dramatic improvement while remaining true to the original mission of our founding sisters. And certainly, remaining true to our mission is the glue that holds us together, the end-all and be-all, if you will—our reason for being.

OUR ROOTS

So I will tell you about a quality journey that began when those five Catholic sisters left their native Germany to "be about God's work." They were led by Mother Mary Odilia Berger, a onetime unwed mother and barmaid. Her passion to form a religious community and to be of service to people in need guided the sisters in those first difficult years. Perhaps passion and the unusual background of this determined woman have shaped SSM Health Care in ways even I can't fathom.

A Sense of Destiny

There's a story that the sisters had planned to sail from Germany on a certain ship, but they arrived late at the port and the ship sailed without them. That ship never made it across the ocean; it sank en route. Of course, the sisters did not know what had happened to the original ship when they boarded the ship that would take them to a new land. They learned of the tragedy

Figure 2   Early photo of Mother Odilia and the sisters.

much later. When I think about that story, I feel a certain sense of destiny—that the sisters were destined to be of service in this country.

The sisters arrived in St. Louis on November 16, 1872, and almost immediately encountered a smallpox epidemic. They began providing nursing care in people's homes. It didn't take long for them to become a familiar and welcome sight as they left their convent each day and walked to the homes of desperately ill people. While four of the sisters visited the sick, Mother Odilia walked the streets begging for food and supplies, not only to feed the sisters, but to help their patients. It was a tenuous beginning, but Mother Odilia had learned how to be a nurse on the battlefields of the Crimean War, and she was determined to use her skills to care for people in St. Louis. Her vision was to provide medical care for anyone who was sick, regardless of race, color, creed, or ability to pay—and that's exactly what the sisters did.

Figure 3   Mother Odilia.

Our First Hospital

As news of the sisters' good works spread, more and more women sought to join the congregation. In 1876, Mother Odilia borrowed the then enormous sum of $16,000 (which translates to millions of dollars in today's terms) to open a hospital, because she believed more people could be served in a hospital setting than in the home. When the hospital was up and running, the sisters welcomed patients who couldn't pay, referring to them in the ledgers as "ODL," or "Our Dear Lord's."

Yellow Fever

When yellow fever broke out in the summer of 1878, first in Memphis, Tennessee, and later in Canton, Mississippi, Mother Odilia received desperate pleas for sisters to nurse the sick. When she asked for volunteers, the sisters willingly stepped forward. Mother Odilia sent 13 sisters—more than one-third of the congregation—to the two cities. By the time the epidemic ended that fall, all of the sisters who had volunteered had

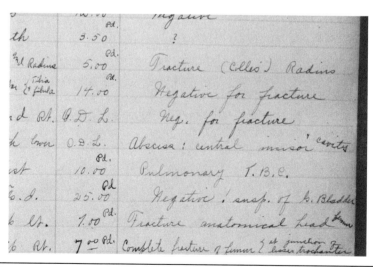

Figure 4 Our Dear Lord's.

become ill with yellow fever and five of them had died. The oldest of those who died was 28 years old.

Forging a Path

Through the remainder of the nineteenth century and all of the twentieth, the sisters cared for people in need, always providing care of the highest quality and always with love. In 1933 in St. Louis, they opened the first Catholic hospital for African-Americans, an act that not only benefited African-American patients, but also gave African-American physicians and nurses a place to practice medicine. Seventy years later, we still hear stories about how the opportunity to practice their profession made a difference in the lives of those doctors and nurses.

The sisters were ahead of their time in many ways. They had never heard the word "diversity," but they lived it. They arrived many decades before the advent of mind–body science, yet they cared for "the whole person—body, mind, and spirit." Long before environmental awareness became a cause, they were committed to the preservation of the earth as well as living in a way that did no violence to the earth. They made quality their quest a century before W. Edwards Deming brought that concept to the attention of the business community.

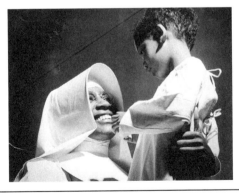

Figure 5   African-American Franciscan Sister of Mary with child.

As its reputation spread, the congregation continued to expand. The sisters had a way of spotting needs and finding ways to meet them. Gradually, they opened more and more

> *The sisters . . . made quality their quest a century before W. Edwards Deming brought that concept to the attention of the business community.*

hospitals, until they were represented in four Midwestern states and South Carolina. In the early part of the twentieth century, they opened nursing schools and began to train young nurses.

MY EARLY YEARS IN HEALTH CARE

My part of the story began in 1960, when I joined the congregation. I grew up in the '50s in a small town in Wisconsin. There were few career opportunities for women in those days, and my family could not afford to send me to college. So I enrolled in a diploma program in nursing at St. Mary's Hospital in Madison, Wisconsin, which was run by the congregation now known as the Franciscan Sisters of Mary—my congregation. A year after

Figure 6 Sister Mary Jean as a young nurse.

I earned my nursing diploma, I entered the convent, and the very next day, I enrolled in the bachelor's of nursing program at St. Louis University. Our sisters have always had a profound respect for education, and I have been blessed with an education far beyond what I could have imagined. After I received my nursing degree, I attended the University of Wisconsin and earned a master's in hospital administration from Xavier University in Cincinnati.

I began my health care career as a nurse and later became an operating room nursing supervisor. Those positions opened my eyes to the realities of the health care environment and ultimately helped shape my determination to make changes. In those very early days, for example, nurses were expected to stand when the doctor arrived at the nursing station. I firmly believe that without this clinical background, I would not have been so passionate about the need to eliminate hierarchies and transform health care.

As the years unfolded, I assumed executive positions with several SSM hospitals until, in 1986, I became president and CEO of the newly formed SSM Health Care. I've been asked if those earlier positions helped shape my commitment

Figure 7 St. Mary's Hospital, Madison, Wisconsin.

to performance excellence. My answer is, "not really." Here's why. When I was a nursing supervisor, my focus was on the moment—on the work being done at the time. The demands of the job were such that I had no opportunity to see the big picture. Stepping into the role of CEO allowed me to see things from a different perspective, and what I realized was that, as a system, we were content to be better than average. Of course, that was unacceptable to me. However, I will be eternally grateful for my experience as a nurse, since it helped me appreciate the myriad challenges faced day in and day out by our caregivers and others in our organization. But back to our path to becoming exceptional.

SOME STORIES

Have I had fun along the way! I remember serving as interim president in the late '70s at a rural Missouri hospital that we'd just taken over from another religious order.

As the hospital's new owner, we were trying to recruit much-needed physicians. When doctors visited, we would host them along with local dignitaries at cocktail parties on the premises. One of my many jobs was to ensure that the bar was fully stocked for these events. One day I mentioned to the food service manager that we needed more gin.

My office in the hospital opened into a large waiting area. One afternoon, the general superior of the congregation that had formerly owned the hospital was seated in that area waiting to speak with me. As she sat there, into the waiting area walked our food service manager, with the biggest bottle of gin I'd ever seen. Holding the bottle high, she looked at me and said, "Sister, your gin's here!"

In a different vein, I remember a story told by some of our sisters who had served at one of our hospitals in the South. They worked in maternity at a time when segregation was the law of the land. During the day, the hospital placed all the white babies in one room and all the black babies in another room. But our sisters were both color-blind and pragmatic. So, to utilize staffing on the night shift, each evening the sisters moved all the babies into one room, where they slept peacefully under the sisters' attentive care. To the best of our knowledge, no baby ever suffered from the experience.

I remember that story when I think about all we've done at SSM Health Care to achieve diversity, and I wonder if it played a role in shaping my determination to change the status quo. We've had to do a lot of work, but we had a tradition that provided the inspiration.

LOOKING IN THE MIRROR

Because our story is about a health care system that challenged the assumption that being better than average was good enough, I've thought a lot about what it is that makes one challenge the status quo. Why do we look in the mirror, so to speak—at our lives or at our organization—and say, "Something's not right"?

The sisters of my congregation, the Franciscan Sisters of Mary, have always had the courage and honesty to look into that mirror. Throughout their history, they have made difficult decisions, even letting go of things that didn't work anymore. At times, that meant selling hospitals or, when the community need no longer existed, even closing them. The decision to let go of something near and dear to us is always painful. That's why it's essential to focus on a broader vision. There will always be difficult and emotional decisions to make, but those decisions will be easier if they are seen in the context of the long-term vision of the organization.

In the latter decades of the twentieth century, my congregation's willingness to ask difficult questions led to the formation of SSM Health Care. Prior to forming the system, the congregation governed its health care facilities through a board made up solely of sisters. Despite the fact that the health care facilities reported to this board, the hospitals defined themselves as individual facilities; there was no sense of unity. In addition, the board had a tendency to manage many of the day-to-day issues rather than govern in a broad sense.

SSM HEALTH CARE

The congregation decided to establish SSM Health Care after the sisters identified two overarching concerns. First, the number of sisters in the congregation was declining, calling into question the future of our health care ministry. Second, the structure they were using to govern our hospitals was not effective.

As an example of the latter, consider the experience of Bill Thompson, who later moved into system management, as executive vice president of our St. Mary's Hospital in Kansas City in the early 1980s. In those days, the governing board had to approve just about anything the hospitals did. Bill wanted to conduct a routine employee satisfaction survey. But he had

Figure 8   Bill Thompson.

to follow the established process, which meant waiting for his monthly trip to St. Louis to present to the sisters. We knew things had gotten out of control when one of the nuns asked Bill, right after his presentation, "Why didn't you just conduct the survey? Why did you bring it to us for approval?" Bill couldn't have agreed more.

We also had a rule in those days that no hospital president could spend more than $5000 (unbudgeted) without the approval of the board. Can you imagine that? Even without inflation, such a restriction would be ludicrous in today's world. And it didn't work very well back then, either.

But it was our reality. The questions we had to ask ourselves were: "How can we make things operate more efficiently? What do we need to control, and what can we let go of? How can decision making be moved to the level where it makes the most sense? (The principle for this is subsidiarity.) And how can we ensure the continuation of our health care ministry when there are no more sisters?" That last question is not unique to SSM Health Care. In fact, as the number of Catholic nuns continues to decline, most Catholic health care organizations are seeking ways to carry on the healing ministries begun by sisters when there are no longer any sisters present in those Catholic facilities.

That last question was also the most difficult. Facing mortality is never easy; we'd all rather operate under the belief that we will defeat the well-established odds and live forever. My congregation's decision to look at reality and make the changes that needed to be made was an act of courage.

Creating the new structure took years. But the sisters' willingness to ask the difficult questions and then take the time to come up with a new course of action has been a model for me in my role as the CEO of SSM Health Care.

The creation of SSM Health Care legally separated the congregation from the hospitals by creating a board of directors

The questions we had to ask ourselves were: "How can we make things operate more efficiently? What do we need to control, and what can we let go of? How can decision making be moved to the level where it makes the most sense? And how can we ensure the continuation of our health care ministry when there are no more sisters?"

to govern the system. For the first time, laypeople participated both on the board and in senior management. Bill Schoenhard and Bill Thompson were appointed to senior management positions, the former as chief operating officer and the latter as a regional vice president.

Today, our SSM Health Care board sticks to its main responsibilities: to keep the organization focused on our vision and to ensure that we meet our communities' needs and remain vibrant. It is my job to run the business and to help the board do its job.

Under our structure, as CEO, I have a great deal of authority delegated to me by the board, so I can make many decisions without seeking approval. Some of these decisions have shaped SSM Health Care in ways I could never have expected.

PRESERVATION OF THE EARTH

For instance, in 2005 SSM recycled some five million tons of material. Every one of our more than 20 facilities has a team that is charged with "preservation of the earth." These teams are made up of employees who are passionate about recycling and about finding creative ways to preserve nature's gifts. When people are passionate, there is no end to their creativity. So through these Preservation of the Earth teams, every one of our hospitals not only contributes to the betterment of its community, but also is faithful to my congregation's commitment to nonviolence.

> *Before I finally slept, I realized that I couldn't clean up Boston Harbor, but I could do my part to make a difference.*

How did this come to pass? In 1989, I was reading *Time* magazine when I noticed a disturbing photograph of Boston Harbor. The harbor was filled with floating trash, including a number of Styrofoam cups. At the time, every SSM facility used Styrofoam, which contains chlorofluorocarbons (CFCs), said by scientists to contribute to the destruction of the ozone layer in the atmosphere. I was so haunted by the photograph that I could hardly sleep that night; the image would not go away. Before I finally slept, I realized that I couldn't clean up Boston Harbor, but I *could* do my part to make a difference. Several days later, I sent a memo to all our presidents banning the use of Styrofoam throughout SSM Health Care. Not everyone was pleased with my decision, but I gave them time to switch to new products, and they complied with my mandate. That was our bold first step toward taking better care of the earth. Not long after, I sent another memo requesting the creation of Preservation of the Earth teams at all our entities.

NONVIOLENT AND INCLUSIVE LANGUAGE

Similarly, inspired by my congregation's commitment to nonviolence, we elected to discontinue the use of violent language as a system and to use inclusive language. Thus, we do not refer to bullet points, but rather to dot points. We do not talk about targets, but rather audiences. We do not blow up a picture; we enlarge it. At the same time, we do not have chairmen of the board, but rather chairpersons. We do not assume a physician is a "he" and a nurse is a "she." And even though we are a Catholic organization, we do not assume that everyone in our organization is Catholic. So when we open a meeting with a prayer, it might be something from a Native American song, the Gospel, or Kahlil Gibran.

PRAYER

Many years ago, as a new vice president at our St. Mary's Hospital in Madison, Wisconsin, I had a new resident named Ron Levy. Ron knew that, as a Catholic organization, we routinely began meetings with a prayer. Ron had been on the job for two weeks when the CEO called on him to say the prayer at the beginning of an administrative council meeting. He quickly passed the assignment on to someone else—actually, a colleague whom he knew was Catholic.

Now, I liked Ron a lot. (I still do.) And sometimes I'm tough with people I like. So after the meeting, I called Ron into my office and asked why he hadn't said the prayer. He explained that to him, prayer was very personal, part of his deep faith, and not something he did in public. I told him: "Ron, I'm not asking you to be Catholic. And I know you've only been here two weeks. So, if you'd like to make it three, I suggest you be prepared to pray the next time you're asked." And Ron's been praying ever since. He's been with our organization for more than 30 years, most recently as president of our St. Louis region.

DIVERSITY

Another example of a decision that shaped our organization has to do with diversity. Our diversity efforts began in earnest on a day in 1997 when a clerical worker at our corporate office pointed out to me that, although we thought of ourselves as a diverse organization, the numbers told a different story. Working with Steve Barney, our senior vice president of human resources, we began an immediate and focused approach to make our organization truly diverse. The appointment of Yvonne Tisdel to the position of corporate vice president–human resources and system diversity led to unimaginable progress. Over the years, we've had everything from theatrical productions to regularly

Figure 9 Steve Barney.

scheduled diversity forums, mentorship programs, vendor diversity fairs, a diversity advisory council, and expanded educational opportunities for minorities. As a result, not only has the number of diverse managers increased significantly in our organization, diversity has become part of who we are, from the

Figure 10 Yvonne Tisdel.

cards sold in our gift shops to the way we care for patients from diverse backgrounds.

Making an executive decision to ban Styrofoam or become diverse was one thing. Moving the organization from better than average to exceptional has been a very different challenge indeed. I'd like to be able to say that I knew the day I became CEO—in July 1986—what our path would be. But, frankly, I didn't have a clue. None of us did.

2

A Conversation over a Beer

Our first step on the journey to move SSM Health Care from good to exceptional can be traced to a conversation over a beer at a swimming pool in 1989. But a lot led up to that conversation.

OUR LEADERSHIP CONFERENCES

The year after my appointment as CEO in 1986, we held the first of what would become annual leadership conferences on Marco Island, Florida. In those years, conference attendance was limited to managers at SSM Health Care. It took us about a decade to understand the huge mistake inherent in this limitation. Today a significant percentage of attendees at our leadership conferences come from every level and every nook and cranny of our organization—from the laundry to dietary to admitting to clinical areas. I view every employee at SSM Health Care as a leader, capable of significant contributions. So it makes the utmost sense to nurture people at all levels of the organization and give them lots of opportunities to hone their leadership skills. More on leadership at all levels later.

*In*trapreneurship

In 1988, the theme of our leadership conference was "*in*trapreneurship," a term that had recently been coined by Gifford

Figure 11   Sister Mary Jean at the 1987 SSM leadership conference.

Pinchot III in his book *Intrapreneuring* (Harper & Row, 1985). Pinchot describes intrapreneurship as a work environment that fosters creativity and invention, even within large organizations. When he observed corporations, Pinchot found employees who willingly spent their creative energy on projects for the good of their companies or institutions. He found people who brought new ideas, products, and services to fruition. We knew that many of our employees also had wonderful ideas for doing things better. Intrapreneurship offered a possible way to transform those ideas into real-world practices. So the questions I posed at our leadership conference that year were: "How could *we* develop that kind of environment? How could SSM foster this kind of creative and innovative approach throughout our large and complex organization?"

Servant-Leadership

At our 1989 leadership conference, we had a new focus: servant-leadership. In his book *On Becoming a Servant-Leader* (Jossey-Bass, 1996), Robert K. Greenleaf tells the story of a group of itinerant monks who were on a long journey to meet their new abbot. One monk tirelessly waited on the others and took care of their needs until, a day or two before the end of the journey, he excused himself and vanished. The others were lost without him, but somehow muddled through. When they arrived at their destination they were stunned to learn that the abbot they had come to meet was the monk who had been their servant.

This story has everything to do with health care. Not only at SSM but in all of health care, people have built their lives around being of service to others. So, servant-leadership became our mantra in 1989.

Flavor of the Month

The problem was that people were confused. Were we doing intrapreneurship or servant-leadership? Employees thought that whatever book senior leaders had read last became the focus for the year. In 1988, we became intrapreneurs—creative and innovative—for a year. In 1989, we would become servant-leaders—with service to others constantly on our minds—for a year.

Despite the success of each year's leadership conference, I began to feel a nagging in the pit of my stomach that told me something wasn't right. I wasn't alone.

And this brings me back to the swimming pool. At the end of our 1989 conference, I sat at the pool with Bill Thompson, who at the time was a regional vice president. As we chatted over a beer, we confided to each other our feelings of unease. It seemed that no matter how much we communicated our mission and values, certain critical things were just not happening. Despite our enthusiasm for various management philosophies, something was missing. It harkened back to my congregation's willingness to look in the mirror.

What we realized was this: Despite all our efforts, we did *not* see the kind of constant striving for improvement we thought we should be seeing. We did *not* see managers mobilizing employees to work on important projects. We did *not* see processes in place that made the best use of people's talents. In short, although we didn't have hard evidence for it—these conclusions were a matter of our subjective perception—we did not seem to be making any genuine effort to be the best. We appeared to believe we were pretty good—and we were content with that. In short, we were complacent.

Although we didn't know it at the time, we realize now that we were doing two things wrong. First, we were a world-class example of the flavor-of-the-month syndrome. How could anyone in our organization focus when we kept changing direction? And second, it was always "we"—the senior executives—who were sending down the truth from the mountaintop to "them"—the employees.

IMPROVING THE COMPLEX
PROCESSES OF HEALTH CARE

As we spoke these thoughts aloud, it became obvious to Bill and me that we had to find some way to tap the vast potential within SSM Health Care. We had to find some process or tool or way of life that would help us improve the hundreds of complex processes that are inherent to health care. And we knew that whatever we did, we had to do it for the long haul—not just for one year.

As Bill and I talked, each of us mentioned that we had been hearing about the success of a new concept called total quality management, or continuous quality improvement (CQI). Although its use was minimal in health care, it was being utilized successfully in business and industry.

I had attended an American Hospital Association meeting in Phoenix, where Dr. Brent James told an impressive story. He had studied a homogeneous group of patients who had all had

> *We had to find some process or tool or way of life that would help us improve the hundreds of complex processes that are inherent to health care. And we knew that whatever we did, we had to do it for the long haul—not just for one year.*

gall bladder surgery. None had serious complications beforehand. The study showed that one physician had the highest patient satisfaction and the lowest costs, and he got patients out of the hospital and home faster than anyone else.

Dr. James asked him what he did differently—what was his magic? The physician explained that he had created a homemade video for his patients that explained, step by step, what was going to happen to them. "When you come to the hospital, we're going to do this and this to get you ready. Then, we're going to do the surgery. The first day, you're going to be really uncomfortable, but we'll give you pain medication to take care of that. The second day, you're still going to be uncomfortable. We'll send you home with enough medication to keep you comfortable because, chances are, you'll be happier at home than in the hospital."

The point was that he had given his patients information about what to expect every step of the way. As a result, his patients were happier, they got out of the hospital more quickly, and it cost everybody a whole heck of a lot less money. I was intrigued. How could we bottle that? How could we provide that kind of exceptional care for *all* our patients?

AN EXPERIENCE IN THE OPERATING ROOM

At the same time, with some frustration I remembered an experience I had had as the operating room nursing supervisor in the late '60s and early '70s. One of our surgeons would schedule his patients at 7:30 on Saturday mornings—at the same time as

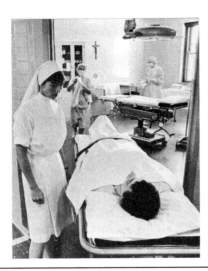

Figure 12   Sister Mary Jean as an operating room nursing supervisor.

Catholic Mass, which he attended religiously, if you'll pardon the pun. How our sisters adored him! "Isn't he wonderful?" they would say to me. I would think about standing around in the OR waiting for him with his patients, who were frustrated at the delay. And I would say, "No! He keeps his patients waiting for him for half an hour! That's not right!" How could we be sure, I wondered, that our patients never experienced this sort of behavior from any physician? What process could prevent this type of delay? Could CQI hold the key?

APPLYING MANUFACTURING PRINCIPLES TO HEALTH CARE

Bill had been reading about the work of W. Edwards Deming, which was having a huge impact on Japanese business. Much of the work was being done in manufacturing, but Bill has always been better than I am at making critical connections. The question he posed was, "Could the same principles that worked so well in manufacturing be applied to health care?"

Bill and I thought they could. We thought that health care processes, like manufacturing processes, could be studied in minute detail and yield important insights. We knew that in health care the devil really is in the details, and that there was a huge variation in how people did things. So back at the corporate office, we put together a team to do some exploration. In the summer of 1989, we met with others who were exploring quality principles in health care settings. The more we learned, the more we were sold on CQI, and the more we believed we should implement it systemwide. But since implementing CQI would be such a major endeavor, we wanted to be sure the board supported us.

CQI: THE JOURNEY BEGINS

I remember vividly the day we presented our proposal to the board. They were skeptical. One member said, "It sounds so mechanical." Another asked, "What does CQI have to do with our values?"

I was frustrated. I knew what CQI could do for SSM Health Care. Why couldn't others grasp it?

There were two lessons in this for me. First, sometimes you're so close to something that you miss the obvious. And second, the greatest gifts often come to us in disguise. Of course CQI fit with our values; we had simply neglected to explain how. In retrospect, I realize the comments of the board pushed us to better define how CQI meshed with our values as an organization. And that critical link became the foundational piece of our CQI educational material. The frustration I experienced at the board meeting was really directed at myself for missing such an obvious point.

The good news is that once we linked CQI to our values, the board understood exactly what we were trying to achieve and why we felt CQI was such a good fit. And so, in 1990, we began a journey to move SSM Health Care from a little better than average to exceptional. I believed it would take us until 1995. Little did I realize that becoming exceptional is a lifelong commitment.

3

CQI: The First
Tentative Steps

I am eternally grateful that I was completely naïve about the work it would take to implement CQI and the obstacles we would encounter. As I mentioned, our journey began that day in 1989 when we stated out loud that we were not as good as we could be. I'll call that point A. Point B was the day not long after when we identified CQI as the means to move us from better than average to exceptional. Getting from point A to point B was relatively easy, in retrospect. Point C was when we implemented CQI across our system—more than 20 hospitals, 3 nursing homes (at the time—we now have 2), and a host of health-related businesses in four states. Point D, in my mind, is achieving exceptional health care.

Yes, innocence is a wonderful thing. Seventeen years after we began CQI, we're beyond point C, and although we're closer to point D, it's taken longer than I had hoped. What I've learned along the way is that, although we may eventually reach point D, we will never be as good as we possibly can be. That would be perfection, which is possible only in heaven. But we will never stop improving.

A NEW LANGUAGE

After our decision in 1989 to implement CQI, we steeped ourselves in the philosophy and vocabulary of continuous improvement. Our objective was to create a culture in which every employee at every facility and at every level of the organization would constantly seek to improve processes—every single day. CQI would not only inspire the engagement of employees, it would provide the tools and techniques necessary to achieve the desired improvement. It seemed so simple.

In the fall of 1989, Paul Plsek, a nationally known consultant, led our system management team through three days of training. Talk about a paradigm shift! It was like learning a new language. Before CQI, we had been inclined to make decisions based on what we *thought* was going on. Now we were going to make them only after we had made an in-depth analysis of the data. And instead of concentrating on *whom*—on individuals—we were going to concentrate on *what*—on the processes. If something went wrong, we weren't going to ask, "*Who* made the mistake? *Who* is to blame?" We were going to ask, "*How* did the *process* break down?" We were going to think in terms of teams and processes, not individuals and tasks.

To teach this language to everyone at SSM, we knew we were going to need a curriculum. But we didn't have one, and the only curriculum we could find had been developed by Florida Power & Light, a far cry from health care. Still, several of our executives visited the company to better understand its program. They were impressed enough to secure the right to use the curriculum, realizing even then that we would have to make extensive changes to something designed for a utility company.

Working with Paul, we designed our own curriculum for three levels of classes: team member, team leader, and team facilitator. To coordinate the education of so many people in our multistate organization, we created the Quality Resource Center (QRC) at our corporate office in St. Louis. The QRC was command central for training the trainers and coordinating the educational sessions that would be necessary to flow CQI throughout our system.

> *If something went wrong, we weren't going to ask, "Who made the mistake? Who is to blame?" We were going to ask, "How did the process break down?" We were going to think in terms of teams and processes, not individuals and tasks.*

SENIOR LEADERS AS TEACHERS

Every member of our system management team went through the training so we could teach it ourselves. The fact that senior managers were among those who actually taught the material sent a clear message about how serious we were about CQI. But system management—fewer than 10 people at the time—could teach only a small fraction of the classes that would be needed to educate everyone. So we recruited educational champions from each facility.

What a wonderful group of people they were. I'll never forget one woman in particular—Sandy Lamer from our St. Francis

Figure 13 Barb Funches teaches a CQI class at our Good Samaritan Regional Health Center in Mt. Vernon, Illinois.

Hospital in Maryville, Missouri, a rural community. With her New England accent and gruff but loving demeanor, Sandy immediately caught on to the potential of CQI to transform our health system. And over the years, she was one of our most passionate educators, teaching CQI classes in just about every one of our facilities. More on Sandy in a later chapter.

We knew that training everyone in the system and implementing teams across the system would not happen overnight. Nevertheless, we introduced CQI with a flourish at our 1990 leadership conference. We had moved from point A—articulating that we were not as good as we could be—to the first stages of point C—beginning to implement CQI—in a year. Life was good. Or so I thought.

A CHANGE IN CULTURE

When we introduced CQI, we were not just introducing another program; we were essentially changing our culture. We were taking the first tentative steps to move us from better than average to exceptional. And some people had a difficult time right from the start—especially applying the concepts to their everyday reality.

For instance, the basic CQI concept "all work is part of a process" is simple, but the processes themselves are often complex. And that makes operating at the process level complex.

Father Jim Krings, the director of mission at our SSM St. Joseph Hospital in Kirkwood, Missouri, is one of our greatest CQI champions. Here's how he explains the concept: "Steps in a process are separate—but interdependent. When one step isn't working, that affects all the others. In CQI, we look at the whole process to find out where it isn't working. We gather and analyze data, determine where the process broke down, and fix it. Then we duplicate the solution across the system, so that the process works in every hospital."

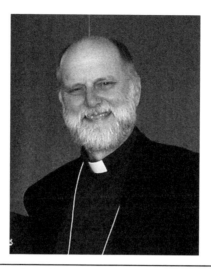

Figure 14 Father Jim Krings.

AN EXAMPLE FROM THE EMERGENCY DEPARTMENT

Nowhere is this easier to understand than in an emergency department (ED), where a series of processes begins the moment a patient comes through the door. If everything goes as it should, the patient moves smoothly from one process to another until he or she is either released or admitted to the hospital. When each activity leads seamlessly to the next, it all works like a well-oiled machine. But anyone who has ever been in an ED understands all too well what happens when processes go awry.

Two of our hospitals (SSM St. Joseph Health Center in St. Charles, Missouri, and SSM St. Joseph Hospital West in Lake St. Louis, Missouri) offer what they call a 30-30 guarantee in their EDs. They guarantee that every person who comes to their ED with a true emergency (chest pain, hemorrhage, and so forth) will be seen by a physician within 30 seconds. All others are guaranteed to be seen by a physician within 30 minutes.

Figure 15   SSM St. Joseph Hospital West.

Part of what is noteworthy about these guarantees is that they are not the result of only a few changes in the EDs. Changes were required throughout the hospitals. For example, in order for patients to be admitted promptly, beds have to be available, so Housekeeping is a key part of the effort. Lab work has to be timely as well. And so on and so on.

If there was one aspect of the new emphasis on process that irritated people the most, it was the concept of "no bad apples." The focus CQI put on correcting processes was interpreted as a kind of denial that certain people really could be inadequate. As time passed, we had to couple our new emphasis on process with the understanding that individuals remain accountable. But this issue still inspires some annoyance.

WORKING IN TEAMS

Process is one key CQI concept; working in teams is the other. Working in teams was familiar to us, but understanding the concept in CQI terms was something new. In health care,

If there was one aspect of the new emphasis on process that irritated people the most, it was the concept of "no bad apples." The focus CQI put on correcting processes was interpreted as a kind of denial that certain people really could be inadequate.

people from different disciplines had always worked together. Interacting as *equals* on interdepartmental teams, however, was another story. With CQI, team facilitators are expected to manage people across the pecking order and, even more difficult, to confront their supervisor or their supervisor's supervisor when necessary. Even more drastic, team members can make decisions that supervisors don't like. Talk about a new way of working that's bound to create emotional stress.

Peter Vrabec, who was one of two original team facilitators at our St. Clare Hospital in Baraboo, Wisconsin, remembers how upset a former director became by the "notion that some workers had more say in a given process than the director" himself. Peter remembers one episode—interesting in part because of how trivial it sounds—where the team

Figure 16   Peter Vrabec.

decided on a new way to dispose of the cardboard boxes in which IV solutions were delivered. It was a method that the director had not approved, and when he discovered the employees using it, Peter says, "I remember him turning several shades of crimson."

Some managers simply couldn't make the transition, Peter recalls. After a while, those managers tended to find positions in other organizations.

Once a team was assembled, it identified a problem, set a measurable goal, and went through a clearly defined process to solve the problem. The process involved collecting data, testing solutions, and monitoring the team's progress along the way. While that may sound fairly straightforward, it wasn't, at least in the early stages of CQI. For one thing, it involved a tremendous amount of conversation about data and technical information. Some people found—and still find—that they lack the appetite for that kind of conversation. Also, hospitals don't operate like manufacturing companies. Jobs take on the stamp of the person who does them, and changes are made by the hour, shift, or day of the week. Tasks are passed from one person to another, often more by spoken word than by written instructions. Eventually, there is so much variation that nothing resembling a process is left.

For instance, the way one nurse administers medication to a patient can differ completely from the way another nurse does. The process becomes highly subjective. In general, we don't think of person-to-person interactions as processes, but they are. Perhaps nurse one introduces herself, finds out how the patient is doing, and asks if there's anything else the patient needs, whereas nurse two abruptly administers the medication without speaking to the patient. We wanted to figure out a way to "bottle" the nurse one interaction.

This meant we had to find a way to identify and analyze our processes. Only then could we hope to improve them. Once again, we drew from other sources—Florida Power & Light and a formula developed by our consultant, Paul Plsek—to create something uniquely our own. We called it the SSM Health Care System Seven-Step CQI Model. The principle is familiar: Determine the customer's needs, and design or redesign the process to meet those needs.

SOME GOOD THINGS

As CQI classes got up and running, some amazing things happened. One of my favorite stories involves a nurse at one of our hospitals who, for whatever reasons, had become extremely negative and was close to being fired. As a last resort, she was asked to attend a CQI team member training session. As she began to recognize her potential to make process improvements, she experienced a genuine transformation. She went on to take team leader training and became a champion of quality improvement. Twenty years later, she still works at that hospital. CQI transformed her.

SOME NOT-SO-GOOD THINGS

But not all experiences were so positive. One example comes from a team formed by our system management—me included—to speed the routing of mail at the corporate office. I believed it was important for senior executives to be on a team to demonstrate to others how a CQI team could generate amazing process improvements. Unfortunately, we struggled for 18 months to no avail. At one point, in our frustration at our lack of progress, we decided the team had too many members, so we voted Bill Thompson and another senior executive off the island, so to speak. What we eventually realized—and this may already be obvious to you—was that in our haste to prove our abilities to use CQI, we had ignored one of its key principles: We had not involved the people closest to the work. Certainly our system management had not a clue about the intricacies

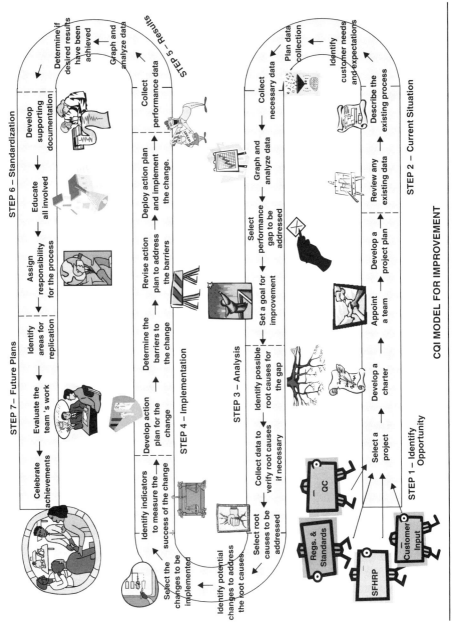

Figure 17 SSM Health Care System Seven-Step CQI Model.

of mail routing. All in all, it was a wonderful lesson, if not a wonderful experience.

Unfortunately, our failed effort pointed to two other problems—problems that were cropping up with teams throughout our system. First, there were no time constraints, so teams like ours were meeting month after month and gathering more and more information with no perspective on when enough was enough, and thus with minimal results. And second, there was no strategic focus to our CQI efforts. Teams could do whatever they wanted. They were asked to identify an "opportunity," which could be anything in any department, from admitting a patient to sending out a bill for services to speeding up mail delivery. Eventually, Baldrige would teach us how essential it is to have a focused approach.

Still another problem didn't seem like one at first. Initially, we were excited about the demand for classes. It seemed like everyone in the system wanted to participate in the training—and we trained them all. The problem was that we didn't have enough team projects for all the people we trained. So people learned the tools and were eager to use them, but they had no way to use their newfound skills. It was a recipe for frustration.

Lynn Widmer is now our corporate vice president of human resources, but for many years she worked at our SSM St. Mary's Health Center in St. Louis, where she taught CQI. Lynn was on the receiving end of a great deal of frustration about the dearth of team projects to accommodate all employees. In Lynn's words: "I would hear that and tell people, 'CQI is not just something you use at work. You can use it in life! I've used it to plan our vacations, to plan my daughter's schedule, and lots of other things. It comes so naturally once you begin to use it.' "

Nevertheless, there was more criticism. Employees claimed that CQI wasn't relevant. SSM Health Care was doing well financially, so why did we need it? I offered a three-part response. First,

Figure 18   Lynn Widmer.

CQI is not an add-on to our work; rather, it is the way we *do* the work. Second, its purpose is to help us deliver better care—and no matter how well we are doing, there is *always* room to improve. Third, exceptional health care goes way beyond finances.

RESISTANCE TO CHANGE

My brilliant answers did not still the complaints. CQI training and teams took time. We were asking very busy people to take hours out of their "regular" jobs to go to classes and participate on teams. In the case of salaried people, who have to work until the job is done, we were adding hours to their week. So it wasn't surprising that many managers and employees saw CQI as extra work on top of already heavy demands. Supervisors complained about scheduling problems. Many asked how we were going to provide coverage for those who attended CQI classes and meetings. Employees, in turn, sensed that supervisors didn't support their team participation. Although these were serious issues, we knew we had intelligent, creative people, and we trusted them to

First, CQI is not an add-on to our work; rather, it is the way we do the work. Second, its purpose is to help us deliver better care—and no matter how well we are doing, there is always room to improve. Third, exceptional health care goes way beyond finances.

solve problems, including how to manage their time. We believed the results would be worth the effort.

Measuring and reporting the results was another important aspect of CQI. Teams were supposed to set goals and track their progress using such tools as flowcharts, graphs, and—most important of all—data. For people who weren't comfortable with numbers, the very word "data" was frightening. But without some kind of objective measurement, we would never know whether we were achieving our goals. Gradually, people became more comfortable with measurement.

CQI AND PHYSICIANS

Among those who were most skeptical about CQI in the beginning were physicians. For many years, their participation on CQI teams was limited. As Dr. Andy Kosseff, medical director of System Clinical Improvement, notes, "Physicians are trained to think, 'I can treat congestive heart failure better than anyone else in my group.' That's the antithesis of CQI."

To promote the approach to physicians, we didn't advertise it as CQI; we called it improving patient care. The first very modest system-level effort came when 3 hospitals—out of 17—participated in a voluntary program to prevent second heart attacks and to reduce mortality in the ones that occur. As Dr. Kosseff will attest, there was plenty of doubt that even this modest effort to reduce variation and bring systematic processes to our treatment methods would pay off. But after a year's work, Dr. Kosseff oversaw a comparison of the relevant mortality statistics from the three hospitals

Figure 19   Dr. Andy Kosseff.

with those from our other hospitals. The results were markedly better at the three that had participated in the program.

This experiment served as a catalyst for physician acceptance of CQI. It showed physicians that by working together, we could achieve substantive improvements in patient care.

CLINICAL COLLABORATIVES

Physician participation also increased with the 1999 launch of our Clinical Collaboratives. These collaboratives involve teams of physicians and other clinicians coming together to focus on a compelling topic—preventing surgical infections, safety, pneumonia, congestive heart failure, critical care, preventing secondary heart attacks—and seeking rapid improvements in that area. We've had remarkable success with these physician-led initiatives, and they have been cited as a best practice by both Baldrige and the Joint Commission on Accreditation of Health Care Organizations.

> *Most physicians work in remarkable isolation. They often have no idea how their hospital performs as a whole—even in their own practice area. So when they are shown data documenting that the hospital's performance is not what it should be, they are both startled and displeased.*

In effect, these collaboratives are fast-track CQI teams devoted to specific clinical areas. In some cases, what has motivated physicians is our sharing with them hospital-wide data they have never seen. Most physicians work in remarkable isolation. They often have no idea how their hospital performs as a whole—even in their own practice area. So when they are shown data documenting that the hospital's performance is not what it should be, they are both startled and displeased.

In other cases, doctors have been reluctant to participate because they're concerned they will be asked to change the way they work. But as Dr. Fil Ferrigni, vice president of clinical affairs at SSM St. Joseph Health Center in St. Charles, Missouri, noted, "Once you present them with the data, with their actual

Figure 20 Dr. Fil Ferrigni.

performance, which shows that they're only doing the recommended intervention, for example, 50 percent of the time, and you provide them with a tool that makes it easy to do the right thing all the time, 99 percent of physicians will run with it."

Our Clinical Collaboratives save lives and make significant clinical improvements, and the physicians who participate know they are making a difference in the lives of their patients. Again, the lessons are that teams must focus on strategic goals, be fast-paced, and produce relevant results. To this day, physician involvement in our Clinical Collaboratives continues to grow, although it still isn't what I think it needs to be.

THINKING DIFFERENTLY

But back to the early '90s. By 1994—four years after we started—the majority of employees had had some experience using CQI. And it had made a difference. "CQI taught us to think differently about what we were doing," says Sister Susan Scholl, president of our SSM St. Mary's Health Cen-

Figure 21   Sister Susan Scholl.

ter in St. Louis and a Franciscan Sister of Mary. "It helped us focus on something as small as how the nursing unit delivers medications to something as overarching as how we communicate when we have patients flowing through the Emergency Department."

Mary Calcaterra, manager of organizational development for SSM Health Care–St. Louis, knew CQI was taking hold when she began to hear employees using the language appropriately—even when senior executives were not around. When Mary heard employees discussing a problem and saying, "Well, let's collect some data," or "Let's map out the process," she knew something had clicked.

Yet something was wrong. In many cases, people still weren't interested in improving. Being better than average was acceptable to them. A malaise still permeated the organization; inertia ruled. In some cases, CQI had actually drained people of energy. With no incentives to achieve rapid results, teams were languishing. We were suffering from paralysis by analysis. Progress had stalled.

These realizations made me more determined than ever to transform our culture. But to move to the next level of quality, I knew we needed a push—a really big push.

Figure 22　Mary Calcaterra.

4

The Baldrige Push

We got that push one day in 1995.
Someone actually asked me if we were still doing CQI. This, I recognized, was my wakeup call. We had to start making some changes. We had to find a way to focus our improvement efforts. We had to achieve results more quickly. We had to demonstrate that the improvement efforts were making a difference in our organization.

I first became aware of the Malcolm Baldrige National Quality Award when Wainwright Industries, a family-owned business from St. Peters, Missouri, received it in 1994. Named after the late secretary of commerce in the Reagan administration, the Baldrige Award is given by the president of the United States in recognition of performance excellence. Originally intended to spur this country's ability to compete in the global economy, it touches every aspect of business: finance, marketing, quality, satisfaction, community outreach, ethics, service, evaluation, and people. In the years since its inception in 1988, it had taken on broad significance and prestige.

Health care organizations would not become eligible to apply for the Baldrige Award until 1999. But not long after Wainwright received the award, Baldrige offered a pilot for health care providers, and we decided to participate. Unfortunately, when we scored ourselves, we did not do well, but our results got us thinking about how we could use the Baldrige process to improve as a system.

STATE QUALITY AWARD PROGRAMS

At the same time, we became aware of the state quality award programs, which were modeled on the Baldrige, and we asked our hospitals to apply in their respective states. Our goal was not to win awards, but to gather feedback to fuel our improvement efforts.

This was an enormous undertaking. At our St. Francis Hospital & Health Services in Maryville, Missouri, for example, the application was handled the first year—1995—by a single employee, who, when she finished, declared, "If you ask me to do that again, I'll quit." We didn't ask her again.

The next year, the hospital formed seven teams of about four to five people each. These people worked hundreds of hours—often until 10:30 or 11:00 at night for about three months—trying to decipher the somewhat ambiguous, cumbersome Criteria and writing—jointly—a 50-page report on hospital processes and operations. They remember praying that they would win so they wouldn't have to apply again anytime soon (the rules forbid winners from applying for three years). They did all this while they were trying to hire a new president, because their president had resigned to take another position at SSM.

A PSYCHOLOGICAL BOOST

But they also remember the excitement of working in teams that cut across functions and hierarchies. They remember the exhilaration they felt when the examiners came for their site visit, because they sensed that they had done a terrific job. And they remember the thrill of learning one afternoon in October 1996 that they had won the Missouri Quality Award. Their little 86-bed hospital in northwest Missouri had been only the second hospital in the state to receive the state quality award from the Excellence in Missouri Foundation.

> *We became aware of the state quality award programs, which were modeled on the Baldrige, and we asked our hospitals to apply in their respective states. Our goal was not to win awards, but to gather feedback to fuel our improvement efforts.*

St. Francis's win, and a similar state quality award for our Bone & Joint Hospital in Oklahoma City, provided a profound psychological boost to our improvement efforts. People throughout our system were thrilled. The long years of CQI, they realized, had not been in vain.

Several more state awards came in quick succession. And whether or not it won, every hospital that applied for a state award received a feedback report containing detailed information about strengths, opportunities for improvement, and its ability to sustain the level of performance it had achieved. Each hospital obtained a vision of itself from the outside and an opportunity to address the issues raised in the feedback. And each hospital became more integrated in its operations, as all functions learned better how they could play a part in seeking excellence. As Rita Miller,

Figure 23   St. Francis Hospital & Health Services, Maryville, Missouri.

community relations director at St. Francis, puts it, "Before this process, those of us in the offices and support systems never thought of quality as a part of our jobs. Now we did."

"It made every employee accountable—instead of just management and administration," adds Kathy Brand, nurse manager of the hospital's medical surgical unit and obstetrics.

AN OPEN CULTURE

Even beyond that, we somehow began to slowly move from an every-hospital-for-itself mindset to a collective perspective. In spite of an initial reluctance to share information from hospital to hospital, we began to understand—as the doctors would begin to do with the collaboratives that came later—that this was the most effective way for all of us to improve. If we worked together to improve, we would all achieve better results than we would operating as separate entities.

Like everything on our journey, creating a climate of openness and willingness to share did not happen quickly—or easily. I'll never forget the first time—it must have been around 1985—we shared hospital-specific financial information at a meeting of hospital presidents and other senior executives. I thought several of the presidents were going to pass out, especially those with less than stellar financial results!

Showcase for Sharing

One of the best things we did to encourage an open culture was to introduce the Showcase for Sharing at our annual leadership conference in 1996. A few months before the conference, we sent invitations to all of our entities, asking each of them to choose a team that had improved a process or had a significant achievement to share with conference attendees.

I'm always inspired by the creativity of the Showcase for Sharing displays at our leadership conferences. Not long ago, the diversity team from our St. Mary's Hospital in Madison,

Figure 24   Showcase for Sharing.

Wisconsin, featured a drummer at its Showcase for Sharing booth, along with information about the English as a second language program and various innovations. The sound of the drumming reverberated throughout the very large room, infusing our conference with energy.

Over the years, we've showcased everything from best practices in safety to significant improvements in clinical care to Preservation of the Earth activities. The Showcase for Sharing at the leadership conference became so popular that we decided to hold it again in the fall. So every year now, people throughout the system gather to share twice: first in May at the leadership conference, and again in the fall for a day of presentations on exceptional achievements. Through the years, I have encouraged participants to "shamelessly steal" Showcase for Sharing ideas and use them in their own facilities.

OUR DRY-RUN BALDRIGE APPLICATION

Our move from a silo mentality to an open culture was a significant step in preparing to apply for the Baldrige as a system. By late 1996, I had determined that the Baldrige would be the best tool to propel our organization to the next step on our journey. The Baldrige application process would enable us to scrutinize our organization in a way we never had before. But, as usual, there was a problem: There was no Baldrige Award for not-for-profit organizations such as health care and education. The Baldrige was exclusively for for-profits: manufacturing and other businesses.

As an ardent proponent of quality in health care, I was very frustrated with the fact that health care was not yet eligible to apply, and I expressed my extreme frustration to the Baldrige Board of Overseers, of which I was a member. Probably more than anyone else, the members of the Board of Overseers expended great effort to have health care and education added to the program. I felt confident that the board would prevail eventually, and I wanted SSM to be ready when health care became eligible. So in 1997, we began to prepare. We took an in-depth look at the Baldrige Criteria, and then we actually completed a Baldrige application that we did not submit—a dry run for the day we knew would eventually come.

Concealed within that last sentence is an enormous amount of blood, toil, tears, and sweat. This book is about our turbulent journey toward excellence. Allow me to say that even *trying to understand the Criteria* of the Baldrige Award was a stomach-wrenching and sometimes mind-numbing experience. The Criteria filled a 70-page book that does not, shall I say, read like a novel.

Allow me also to say that asking our people to undertake an entire Baldrige application for, in a sense, *nothing*—for a dry run—took a lot of what many people would describe with such words as *chutzpah, gall, sadism,* or a particularly virulent combination of all three. Applying for the Baldrige involved dozens of people doing hundreds and hundreds of hours of work—all on top of their regular jobs. Asking them to do it as a dry run was a bit like ordering them to train for a triathlon on top of their day jobs—and telling them that on the day of the competition, they would be spectators.

So I am sure my popularity was not enhanced by this request. But such are the joys of leadership, and as the saying goes, "No pain, no gain."

It soon became apparent that even if it was all a dry run, the Baldrige Criteria were going to help us—even before we filled out the application. That's because after studying the Criteria, we realized they were not going to tell us *how* to run our organization, but rather that they would help us determine whether we were actually doing what we said we were doing.

MIND THE GAPS

And we quickly found several gaps, most of them fairly easy to address. Not so easy, however, was the absence of a mission statement for our entire organization. Don't get me wrong: We were not without words about our mission. Our problem was that we had *21 pages* of mission statements from across the system. In addition, our *system* mission statement was 85 words long—and, in the grand corporate literary tradition, it was the product of a corporate office committee.

As we agonized over this situation at a system management meeting, Ron Levy, president of SSM Health Care St. Louis, uttered the fateful words: "Do you think maybe we need a single mission statement?" Once those words had been spoken aloud, we knew he was right, and that somehow we needed to cut a path, like Ernest Hemingway, through the impenetrable rain forest of language we had created.

In 1998, we began a yearlong process to develop a single system mission statement. Mission statements have existed for as long as organizations have existed. Mission statements are what an organization is about—why it exists. So having 21 pages of mission

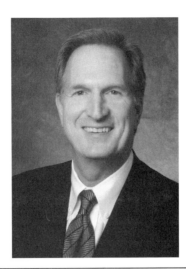

Figure 25   Ron Levy.

We had 21 pages *of mission statements from across the system. In addition, our* system *mission statement was 85 words long—and, in the grand corporate literary tradition, it was the product of a corporate office committee.*

statements underscored the fact that we lacked the kind of focus we needed to become a world-class health care organization.

Because we took the creation of a mission statement extremely seriously—we regarded it as the single most important initiative we had ever undertaken as a system—I'll go into our work in depth in the next chapter. But for now I will disclose this: Our mission statement is now 13 words long.

HOW THE BALDRIGE APPLICATION WORKS

But back to the Criteria and our 1997 dry-run application. Back then there were seven Baldrige categories by which applicants were judged:

1. Leadership

2. Strategic Planning

3. Customer and Market Focus

4. Information and Analysis

5. Human Resource Development and Management

6. Process Management

7. Business Results

There are still seven categories, although the terminology has changed over the years. In each category, the Criteria pose very specific questions. For instance, in the Leadership category the questions include: How does the organization discern and frame what is important to it? How does the organization communicate and deploy its mission and values throughout the enterprise? Strategic Planning questions include: How does the organization convert its objectives into action plans? How do strategic and action plans link to the performance management process? What does the organization do if circumstances require a sudden shift in plans? And under Information and Analysis, some questions are: Why does the organization collect the information it collects? How does the organization use data to drive decision making?

These questions may not seem hard. But believe me, answering them is.

Each category is assigned a certain number of points, up to a maximum of 1000. Trained Baldrige examiners review the applicant's information and assess the organization's approach, deployment, learning, and integration in each category. An initial team of examiners (usually 8 to 10 people) reads and scores the application independently. If the score is high enough, the applicant goes to consensus review, and another team of six to eight people reviews the application to develop a consolidated, consensus-based feedback report.

This report goes to a panel of judges, which votes on which applicants get site visits.

Results and processes go hand in hand. Even if the results are great, an organization has to demonstrate that it understands the processes by which they've been achieved. In some instances, we had great results, but we could not link our results to a process. On the other hand, at times we were strong on process but unable to achieve the results we sought.

Using the information supplied by the field, we developed our dry-run application at the system level. A member of system management led each of the seven teams; I led the leadership team. Later, a review provided scrutiny at both the facility and system levels. Through this back-and-forth process, we stumbled through our first attempt at an application. It was a massive undertaking that involved hundreds of hours on the part of dozens of people.

But it helped prepare us for the next step on our journey: our mission statement.

5

Our Mission

It took a village to write our system's mission statement. The process involved some 3000 employees, took nearly two years from the initial meeting to the day we rolled out the mission at our facilities, and was worth every bit of the time and energy it took to create it. Employees embrace it. People outside SSM find it inspiring. The Baldrige examiners cited it as a "best practice" the year we received the award. Other organizations ask if they can steal it (the answer is no). Patients have actually chosen an SSM hospital because they saw our mission and values displayed on a wall.

In short, the oft-ridiculed process of developing a mission statement was so important to our progress that I wanted to set aside a whole chapter to recount the development and deployment of our mission statement.

> *Patients have actually chosen an SSM hospital because they saw our mission and values displayed on a wall.*

ARTICULATING WHAT ALREADY EXISTED IN PEOPLE'S HEARTS

When we began the process of articulating our mission in 1998, we knew that a deep sense of mission already existed at the

Figure 26 The lobby at SSM Health Care's corporate office in St. Louis.

heart and soul of the organization. Certainly Mother Odilia and those early sisters understood that they were doing the work of God by meeting the health needs of their times. But over the years, as our organization grew and established discrete hospitals, each hospital had created its own mission statement. And even when we formed SSM Health Care in 1986, the system mission statement, which was written by a corporate office team, was 85 words long. Who could remember it? Who could be inspired by it?

Our task in 1998 was to take all the existing mission statements, put them together in one pot over a high flame, bring them to a boil, stir, let them simmer over time as the flavor deepened, and, finally, put the liquid through a sieve to create a highly seasoned broth.

In non-cooking terms, here was the process we used.

THE MISSION DEVELOPMENT PROCESS

In early 1998, we assembled a design team of 75 people, including representatives from all levels at every facility, system management, and our sponsoring congregation—a very big team with a very big job. There was only one criterion for inclusion: a passion for the task.

The team began by putting together a set of assumptions to guide its work. First, the mission statement would describe what we do and what was most important to us. Second, we would not create anything new but would bring to light what was already there. Third, whatever the group came up with would be *the* mission of every SSM facility, regardless of its location, size, or services provided. Fourth, the finished product had to convey not only our purpose but also our passion. It had to inspire. *My* only requirement was that the mission statement be short—no more than one sentence—so even *I* could remember it.

DEEP CONVERSATION

The design team asked the mission director at each of our facilities to hold focus groups to engage in "deep conversation." The corporate office provided training and a script for the focus group leaders. The conversations were structured around specific questions: "What business are we in? How do you understand our mission? What are we passionate about? What values best express what we stand for? If circumstances were to change, and we were penalized for these values, would we keep faith with them—no matter what?" The answer to this last question was an overwhelming yes. Over and over people said they worked at SSM Health Care because of our compassion and our commitment to people who are poor and sick.

The focus groups included individuals from all levels at each facility. A CEO might be seated next to a person from the laundry or someone from admitting, and a nurse might sit next to a lab technician or a food service worker. It was those multiple perspectives that led to some startlingly honest discussions.

I remember an "aha" moment for our communications vice president, Suzy Farren, as to the link between personal values and organizational values. During a focus group, Suzy talked about growing up in rural New Jersey in the early '60s. Every Friday, her mother would join a group of other women for lunch. One Friday, as they ate at the restaurant of a hotel, they heard a commotion. In the lobby were five or six African-American actors (including the acclaimed Ossie Davis and Ruby Dee) who were scheduled to perform in a play at the local theater. They had reserved rooms at the hotel, but when they arrived, they were told they could not stay there. Suzy's mother was outraged. Immediately she arranged to have the actors stay at her home and the homes of the other women at the lunch. The actress Gloria Foster stayed with Suzy's family, and Suzy's mother never set foot in the restaurant again.

Her mother's commitment to human values shaped Suzy's values. As we began to articulate SSM's values in the focus groups, Suzy began to understand how her own values were remarkably similar to the values of SSM Health Care.

Figure 27 Suzy Farren.

GETTING TO THE ESSENCE

The focus group conversations were held over a period of about four months, throughout the spring and summer of 1998. A subcommittee of the design team sifted through thousands of responses, looking for trends. Many of the same words—*excellence . . . exceptional . . . quality . . . respect . . . community . . . integrity . . . teamwork . . . stewardship . . . fiscal responsibility . . . compassion . . . outstanding . . . God . . . faith*—were repeated over and over. After the subcommittee refined the material into words and phrases that encapsulated the essence of the feedback, the design team asked each entity to conduct a second round of focus groups to validate the initial findings. These second focus groups, held in the fall of 1998 and the winter of 1999, confirmed that the design team was on the right track.

Next the design team divided into a smaller group of about 15 people, all with different skills but with solid backgrounds in communications. Half of the group focused on the mission and half on the values. The groups finished their task in the summer of 1999, just weeks before we learned we would become the first health care organization to receive a Malcolm Baldrige National Quality Award site visit.

PRESENTING THE MISSION TO THE BOARD

When I first saw our mission statement and our values, I thought, *This is it.* This is absolutely *it!* But there was one more step before we announced our new mission and values throughout the organization. I wanted to present the documents to the board to see the reaction. As we prepared for the board meeting, I remembered our experience with CQI nine years earlier. What if the board didn't like the mission and values? Would we go back to the drawing board, or would we move forward with the documents that seemed so perfect for our organization?

With my heart in my throat, we sent our new mission state-ment and values to the board members along with the agenda for our September 1999 SSM Health Care corporate board meeting.

Our mission: *Through our exceptional health care services, we reveal the healing presence of God.*

Our values:

Compassion: *We reach out with openness, kindness, and concern.*

Respect: *We honor the wonder of the human spirit.*

Excellence: *We expect the best of ourselves and one another.*

Stewardship: *We use our resources responsibly.*

Community: *We cultivate relationships that inspire us to serve.*

I'll never forget what happened when the agenda item came up at the meeting, and I read our mission and values aloud to the board. When I was done speaking, there was utter silence. No one spoke. As the seconds turned into what seemed like years, I worried that we were so far off base that no one knew what to say.

Finally, Sister Marilyn Jean Davis, one of our board mem-bers, broke the silence. "That is the most profound thing we've ever done," she said. The rest of the board agreed.

As inspiring as the thirteen words of our mission statement are, I am even more inspired by the way in which they came to life. Involvement from people at every level of our organization and at every facility produced a sense of ownership we never could have achieved had we written the materials at the corporate office.

THE ROLLOUT

The next challenge was the rollout. How would we cel-ebrate our mission and values and communicate them in a

> *As inspiring as the thirteen words of our mission statement are, I am even more inspired by the way in which they came to life. Involvement from people at every level of our organization and at every facility produced a sense of ownership we never could have achieved had we written the materials at the corporate office.*

way that was meaningful to employees? Again, we formed a team tasked with developing educational sessions and creating materials for all employees and volunteers. The official launch was April 11, 2000, which seems like a long time after our presentation to the board. But after such a lengthy process to develop the mission, we did not want to be hasty in communicating it.

Every facility held parties to which all employees were invited. Hospital presidents presented the new mission statement and values. We had brochures for everyone in the system, along with wallet-sized cards; we had wall plaques, mugs, and a host of materials proclaiming our mission and values. Little did I realize at the time that this was our very first attempt to deploy a consistent message throughout the organization. We still had much to learn about message deployment.

Much of what we did was very good. For instance, we produced a reflective video to communicate our mission and values. In the video we told a story, the same story that we printed on the wallet-sized cards given to every employee.

The day had been too much. A baby had died in her mother's arms. A man had arrived at the hospital only to find that his wife had died. A young mother of three was diagnosed with cancer. Most days, the joy outweighed the pain. But not that day.

"Why?" the nurse asked God. "Why don't you send help?"

"I did," God replied. "I sent you."

Figure 28   Mission brochure.

This story helped underscore the sacred nature of our mission and pointed out the essential role of employees in their work— no matter what the nature of that work.

Another key element of the mission rollout was a two-hour program for all employees, held after the initial celebration.

The sessions offered employees an opportunity to explore the mission and values in relation to their jobs. We asked each facility to provide enough meetings so all employees could attend one. Facilitators asked questions such as, "When have you revealed the healing presence of God in your job?" and "When did you see someone reveal the healing presence of God—either at work or outside of work?" People were reluctant to talk about themselves, but they were eager to talk about others. As employees shared personal stories, they reconnected to the reasons they had gone into health care in the first place: to make a difference in people's lives.

STORIES OF COMMITMENT AND HEALING

One story came from one of our home care nurses. Jeanette worked with Alzheimer's patients, and she had begun caring for an elderly gentleman whose health had declined rapidly. Soon he forgot how to walk, and he became confined to a wheelchair. But Jeanette knew that inside this man resided a determined spirit and a love of music. She refused to give up on him, and she did something wonderful. She tells it this way: "I wanted him to get some physical exercise, and I knew he wouldn't walk. So every time I went to his house, I would put on music, and we would dance." To me, that story is about Jeanette's persistence in doing whatever she could to give her patient the very best care possible. He needed exercise, and by using her creativity, Jeanette called on something deep within him—some memory etched in his soul. When I think of Jeanette dancing with her patient, I see the healing presence of God.

Another story was about John, a lab employee who for years had quietly been giving roses from his garden to various people in the community. Whether the occasion was happy or sad, John hoped his roses would let someone know that they were in his thoughts. It made him feel good to see others smile. He gave them to colleagues, to patients, and to clerks and checkers at the grocery store.

In the mission rollout meeting at our Maryville, Missouri, hospital, someone described how John's gift of a rose had revealed the healing presence of God. One by one, people in the room spoke about a time John had given them a rose or when they'd seen him giving one to a patient. In the meeting, John sat with his eyes cast down. Finally he began to weep. He had never realized what a difference his simple gift had made in the lives of so many people.

As story after story was told by employees and physicians, we realized that our newly articulated mission statement did not inspire these stories. Rather, it was our employees' commitment and their desire to reveal God's healing that had inspired our mission statement.

The mission rollout meetings continued throughout 2000. When they ended, it was by no means the end of our mission story. But back to Baldrige.

6

Applying for the Baldrige— Three Times, No Charm

As a result of our dry run in 1997, we were better equipped to understand the Baldrige Criteria when health care became eligible to apply for the award in 1999. We decided early on to include all of our entities in a systemwide application. People asked me why we didn't just pick our best hospital, which would have involved far less work and given us a much better chance of winning. My response was twofold. First, it was not about winning, it was about getting better—and that applied to every facility in the system. Second, I was not about to alienate 19 of our 20 hospitals by selecting the one I thought was the "best."

I'll never forget Ron Levy's attitude about applying for the Baldrige in those early years. He was not happy. In Ron's words: "When we started applying for Baldrige, most people fell into one of four categories: agnostics, cynics, believers, and zealots. When I became president of the St. Louis region in December 1999, we had lost $20 million that year. Baldrige, for me, was going to be a lot of work and a distraction from what I needed to do. I was a cynic; and while I am not yet a Baldrige zealot, I have become a Baldrige believer."

THE NUN AND THE NICE JEWISH GUY

Not long after we received the Baldrige in 2002, Ron and I spoke to a group of St. Louis business leaders about how

Baldrige had helped us improve in all areas of our business, including financially (for SSM St. Louis, the turnaround was substantial—around $50 million). The *St. Louis Business Journal* ran an ad for the event that we developed. The headline read: "Find Out What Happens When a Nun and a Nice Jewish Guy Work Together." Although Ron wasn't thrilled about the ad—he's actually not that nice (just kidding)—he certainly was pleased to talk about how he had become a Baldrige convert. My question was, why didn't the ad describe *me* as nice?

Figure 29 "Nun and nice Jewish guy" ad.

OUR FIRST TRY

Beginning in 1999, we applied for four consecutive years. There is no way to describe how much preparation was involved in our first application or how much we learned from the process. We spent many weekends writing and rewriting the application, often encountering a problem that was totally unexpected. For example, after putting hours and hours into preparing a particular category, we would find that the file was corrupt or had disappeared completely. Or, after we had gathered and entered all the data for what we thought was a systemwide practice, we would realize that not all of our entities were actually doing it. For example, after we wrote under "Category 5, Staff Focus" that all of our entities had a Retreat Day for employees (a system policy), we learned that this was not so in every hospital. We made sure that by the time we submitted our application, all our hospitals had instituted a Retreat Day.

As we wrote and rewrote, lights went on all over the place. In that first application, we began with five different customers; gradually, we realized our ultimate customer was the patient. Only then were we able to focus sharply on what we needed to do to serve that customer.

Insight came in other ways as well. One of the best was the site visit.

The Site Visit

Getting a site visit is considered high recognition in the Baldrige world because it indicates that the organization has received a certain number of points for the written application. The purpose of the site visit is to verify and clarify what has been written in the application. We were fortunate to get visits in 1999, 2001, and 2002. These are anything but cursory examinations. In 2002, for example, the examiners visited all of our entities, either in person or by teleconference, and talked to nearly 800 people.

In 1999 it was all new to us. We told employees to relax and answer questions as honestly as they could. When one of the examiners asked a housekeeper at one of our hospitals how he knew he was doing a good job, he responded: "Lady, look at this floor. You can see your face in it. That's how I know I'm doing a good job." Was that the right answer? I don't know, but I thought it was terrific.

I remember another story from our first site visit—again involving Ron Levy. In our application, we had explained that every employee in SSM Health Care had what we call a "passport." I'll discuss them more later, but these passports list every employee's individual goals for their day-to-day work. As it turned out, the examiners decided to visit a physicians office in rural Missouri to be sure that the physicians actually had passports. Ron called ahead and discovered they didn't. So he grabbed a bunch of passports, got in his car, and raced the 50 or so miles to the physicians office to deliver the goods—one step ahead of the examiners.

Another story from our 1999 application process that comes to mind is not funny. Shortly after we learned that we would receive a site visit, we discovered that someone was embezzling money in our SSM St. Louis office. The police made an arrest. Later, the man was convicted and sent to jail, but at the time we were not sure whether we should withdraw our application because of the potential scandal. We decided that it was best to let Baldrige decide how we should proceed, so I made a very difficult phone call. The Baldrige people thanked me for my honesty and told me the site visit would go on as scheduled, because we had taken appropriate action.

Regrettably, we did not yet have our new mission statement when we applied in the spring of 1999. But we did by the time of the fall 1999 site visit, and we couldn't stop talking about it

Figure 30 Passports.

When one of the examiners asked a housekeeper at one of our hospitals how he knew he was doing a good job, he responded: "Lady, look at this floor. You can see your face in it. That's how I know I'm doing a good job." Was that the right answer? I don't know, but I thought it was terrific.

to the examiners. We believed that it beautifully and concisely combined the heritage of our early sisters with our quest to be exceptional. I'm not the most effusive person in the world, but even I couldn't stop rattling on about it.

Our Biggest "Aha" Moment

And then we got our Baldrige feedback. It was our biggest "aha" moment in what became four years of Baldrige applications. The examiners acknowledged that our mission statement was indeed great—exceptional, even. But they asked us two questions: "What do you mean by 'exceptional'?" And, "If you want to be exceptional, why are you content to compare yourselves to the average?"

Those two questions stopped us in our tracks. Collectively, we hit our heads and—to put it in terms any teenager could understand—said, "Duh!" Once again, the glaringly obvious had reared its ugly head, and we had been too close to see it.

What the examiners were saying was, "Great mission statement. Love it. But what does it mean? How do you define it? How do you measure it?"

BACK TO THE DRAWING BOARD

After some serious introspection, we decided on a course of action. We devoted our 2000 strategic planning meeting to defining "exceptional" and figuring out how to measure it. Clearly this was senior management's role—to set the direction and establish systemwide goals. The meeting was attended by system management and the presidents of all of our hospitals. We knew we also needed input from other experts, so we invited representatives from our medical staffs, nurse executives, and human resources and finance departments. And we made it clear that no one could leave until our task was accomplished.

The question we put to the group was simple: "What do you see as the components of exceptional health care services?" After a long, arduous—"torturous" actually seems fair—discussion, we emerged with something concrete and measurable. Exceptional health care services, the group determined, have five characteristics: exceptional clinical outcomes; exceptional patient, employee, and physician satisfaction; and exceptional financial performance.

That was a good beginning, but it led to more questions. How would we *know* when we were delivering exceptional health care services in each of those areas? How could we measure results?

Some measurements, we knew, were fairly straightforward. In the area of financial performance, for example, we had always looked at operating margins to determine whether we had achieved best-in-class levels.

> *Exceptional health care services, the group determined, have five characteristics: exceptional clinical outcomes; exceptional patient, employee, and physician satisfaction; and exceptional financial performance.*

For patient satisfaction, we had patient surveys and a complaint management system, although in 1999 it was far less centralized than it is today. For physician satisfaction, we had physician surveys, and for employee satisfaction, we had employee surveys. Using the data from these surveys and looking at other best practices—both within and outside health care—we determined that we would be able to set specific and measurable goals for patient, physician, and employee satisfaction for a three-year period.

The element we struggled with most was exceptional clinical results. Like any large and complex health care organization, we have clinical results for thousands of different procedures. Moreover, in 1999, clinical results from other health care organizations were not easily accessed. So we kept looking for a single way to measure something very complex. How could we find one indicator for clinical performance that was relevant, meaningful, and measurable at every one of our hospitals? Ultimately we settled on unplanned readmissions within 30 days. In other words, how many patients returned to our hospitals within 30 days of an initial visit? Could we, through process improvements, lower the number of these unplanned readmissions, which were highly distressing to patients?

When the meeting ended, clinicians were not happy. In our quest for something meaningful and universal, we had chosen a measurement that none of our hospitals was exploring and that wasn't even in the literature. Eventually we replaced this goal—but not for several frustrating years.

The other milestone we achieved at the meeting was a determination that we would weigh all five "exceptionals" equally. This was heresy in health care in 1999. Everything, just those few short years ago, was measured in terms of finances. How could employee satisfaction and physician satisfaction have equal weight with financial performance?

Today our decision looks farsighted. But as I look back from today's vantage point, I see how dense we were in not understanding the links among all five of the exceptionals. If there was a problem in one area, it would show up in another. We just didn't realize that at the time.

To be sure we were setting our goals appropriately, we had to identify national best practices and established benchmarks for each of the exceptionals. We had never set goals at the system level in any area other than financial. Baldrige had pushed us to break new ground, and this was only our first application.

IF AT FIRST YOU DON'T SUCCEED . . .

We applied for a second time in 2000. This was probably our weakest application because we hadn't worked on making real improvements; we had simply updated and resubmitted our 1999 application. That didn't hurt us with the 2000 examiners—they'd never seen our 1999 application—but something else did. There were so many more applicants in the health care category in 2000 that the bar was raised. What was good enough to get us a site visit in 1999 was not good enough in 2000.

We learned an important lesson from that. We learned that we needed to make real organizational improvements, not just tweak the prior year's application. The competition was getting better all the time.

In May 2001, we submitted what we considered to be our strongest application yet, and we received another site visit. The visit began with a Sunday dinner between the examiners and key participants. The examiners spent Monday through Thursday morning talking to employees and conducting interviews with appropriate people to verify and clarify that we were doing what we claimed to be doing in our application. For us, this meant that the examiners split up into smaller groups and traveled to different regions. After the visit ended at the corporate office on Thursday around noon, the examiners went back to their hotel to write the feedback report and come to a consensus on key findings. Their report was then submitted to the panel of judges for review and award consideration.

By 2001, employees were relatively comfortable with having people walk around asking questions. With what we considered to be a strong application, a deeper understanding of the Criteria, and a second site visit, we thought we had a pretty good chance of receiving the award. We tried to have fun with the visit. I remember that Laura Jelle, quality director at St. Clare Hospital in Baraboo, Wisconsin, dubbed herself the "queen of quality" and arranged for a red carpet to be rolled out for the examiners when they arrived. Laura herself donned a red cape, tiara, and white gloves for her walk down the carpet. She has never lived that down.

But it didn't work. After considerable suspense, we were notified at 5 p.m. on a Friday that we had not been selected

Figure 31   Laura Jelle, the "queen of quality."

for the award. Nor had anyone else in health care, we learned, although several educational organizations had been named winners for the first time. We asked ourselves what we were missing. What didn't we understand?

THE FEEDBACK

We waited to get our feedback report, and when it arrived in mid-December, we pored over its 50 pages to find clues as to what we needed to do to improve. We looked for things we could work on immediately and things we could do over the next year that would have the greatest systemwide impact. We knew from experience that we had to choose opportunities for improvement that linked to our strategic goals—the five exceptionals.

After we determined what we could do immediately and what would take more time, we had a conversation about whether we should skip a year before reapplying in 2002. Some people felt we needed time to make substantive changes, particularly in the area of clinical results. We had submitted applications three years in a row. People were tired. They couldn't keep up the pace for another year.

I understood that, but I worried that if we took a year off, we would lose momentum. We needed to keep moving forward and accelerate our rate of improvement.

It isn't comfortable creating huge challenges for an organization. But sometimes that's part of a CEO's job, and, more importantly, we owe it to our patients to never let up in our quest to provide exceptional health care services. I knew Baldrige was pushing us out of our comfort zone, but I thought that was exactly the point. We needed to be pushed. So I overruled the people who recommended we take a break, and we went to work to improve our results and apply again in 2002.

We had submitted applications three years in a row. People were tired. They couldn't keep up the pace for another year. I understood that, but I worried that if we took a year off, we would lose momentum. We needed to keep moving forward and accelerate our rate of improvement.

7

Making the Connections

One of our clear challenges was to establish a direct "line of sight" from each employee's everyday work to our mission statement. It was one thing to say that our large and complex organization provides exceptional health care services; it was obviously quite another to help employees understand how they could contribute to that mission. We learned that we were not above stealing to achieve that understanding.

PASSPORTS

We had learned at a 1997 Showcase for Sharing session that our hospital in Maryville, Missouri, had implemented what it called a "passport" program. Each employee would set goals for their work and write them down on a small paper passport that could be attached to their badge. It was a visual reminder to stay focused on what was important.

We stole the idea and implemented passports systemwide in 1998, a couple of years before we established goals around the five exceptionals. In retrospect, we had put the cart before the horse because we had not yet realized how to channel the efforts of everyone in the system toward specific goals. So for several years, people had passports, but the potential of these tiny cards was not realized.

KNEE BONES, THIGH BONES: IT'S ALL ABOUT ALIGNMENT

Once we had set system goals around the five exceptionals, we understood the organizational focus that would be necessary to achieve them. We asked each of our regions to set measurable and specific goals that would further the system's goals. Subsequently, the facilities set measurable and specific goals to further the regional goals. If this sounds like the old song, "The knee bone's connected to the thigh bone . . ." that's exactly how it was—and is.

Much of the alignment was in place, but there was still a gap. It was a big stretch from employee passports to facility goals. We had to come up with a way to link the two. We also wanted to be certain that every department in our system had the focus necessary to achieve the facility's goals.

DEPARTMENT POSTERS

What was missing was a department-level tool. To close the gap, we came up with department posters. A department poster is a simple graphic description of the connections among system, region, entity, and department. The poster visually demonstrates how each level of the organization supports the next level. At the top of the poster is our mission statement. Below that are the system goals for the five exceptionals. The poster contains ample space for the entities to fill in their goals for the five exceptionals and then for each department to fill in the department goals.

Once we determined that the poster/passport process was the tool we would use to deploy our mission, we had to figure out how to communicate the process to everyone in the system. It was especially critical that department managers understood how it worked.

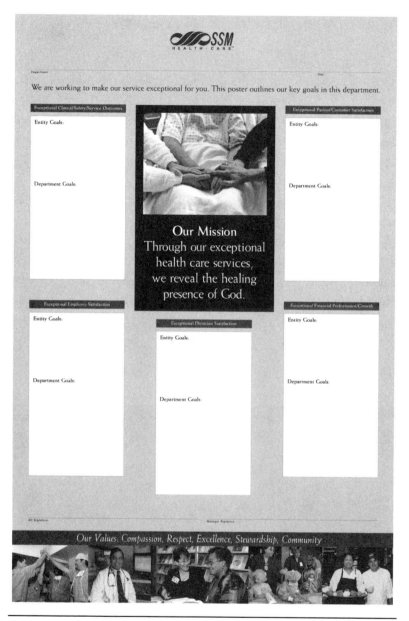

Figure 32   A department poster.

MEETING IN A BOX

So we created the "Meeting in a Box." Our first Meeting in a Box included several items: a video message from me describing the poster/passport process and explaining why it was so important, a PowerPoint presentation with a script to help the manager explain the poster/passport process to employees, and tips on setting goals. We included sample passports and posters in the "box," which was actually a thick plastic folder.

The Meeting in a Box ensured the deployment of a consistent message throughout our large and complex organization. Managers were required to hold sessions for their employees. We required employees to sign in so we were certain they had attended the session. The sign-in was the element that had very often been missing in some of our early deployment efforts.

Every year we produce a new Meeting in a Box, based on feedback we receive from the previous year. There's always

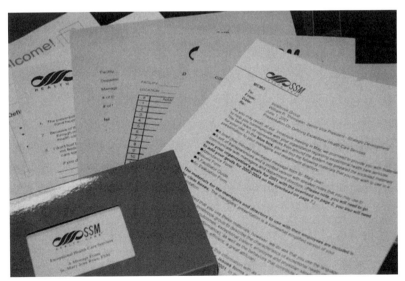

Figure 33　Meeting in a Box.

something that needs to be clarified, restated, or reinforced, and we revise the materials accordingly. We've been producing the Meeting in a Box since 2000, and although the posters and passports get better every year, there is always ample room for improvement. Early on, employee goals tended to be vague. Employees wrote things like, "I will smile more." Whenever I saw this on a passport during my site visits, I would ask the employee, "What does 'more' mean? How will you know when you've smiled more?" Of course, the larger issue is that while smiling is a wonderful thing, much needed in this world, smiling may not mean that much to someone who desperately needs help getting to the bathroom. What they want is a quick response. The point is, we need to do what matters most to our patients.

Department managers use a variety of methodologies to determine what matters most to patients and other customers, and they set department goals accordingly. For example, in our oncology units, we know that pain control is the top priority for patients. A department goal might be to ensure that 100 percent of patients receive pain control assistance before they experience pain. When the department achieves this goal, it helps the entity achieve its goal for patient satisfaction. We have a moral imperative to do the things that matter most to our patients. Many people come to us frightened and confused. We must do everything humanly possible to ease their pain and respond to their concerns.

Employees work with their managers to develop individual goals that are written on their passports, and these individual goals support the department goals. For instance, an individual goal in the oncology unit might be, "I will anticipate the pain control needs of my patients 100 percent of the time." By filling out passports, employees give a concrete expression of their contribution to the overall performance of our organization. These individual goals are a direct connection to our mission and answer the question, "How do I, as an individual, contribute to revealing the healing presence of God?" This is a very powerful way for people to understand how important they are to SSM.

Tom Langston, our chief information officer and president of the SSM Information Center, describes the process: "As the head of the Information Center, I sit down with each of my managers and discuss our goals. The managers write their individual goals on their passports. They, in turn, go through the same process with their employees. That's how individual employees see how they contribute to the mission."

REVEALING THE HEALING PRESENCE OF GOD

There are countless examples of revealing the healing presence of God, but one of the most touching concerns our Footprints^{SM} program at SSM Cardinal Glennon Children's Medical Center in St. Louis. Footprints is a program for the families of children who most likely will not live to adulthood. It's an amazing program with an amazing team of caregivers. Each family is assigned a

Figure 34   Tom Langston.

team that includes a physician, a nurse, a pastoral caregiver, a social worker, and other caregivers appropriate to the family's specific situation. Every time the child comes to Glennon for care, that same team attends to the patient and family. Repeated explanations of the child's condition are not necessary, because the team understands the needs of the child and the needs of the family. Families find the approach incredibly healing.

Not long ago, Footprints had a 17-year-old patient who had had a brain tumor for nine years. She was a straight-A student even though she had spent a good part of her time in the hospital. What she wanted more than anything else before she died was to graduate from high school with her class. But she was in very serious condition and her health was deteriorating rapidly. She was on a ventilator and unable to stand. It didn't seem possible that she would ever leave Glennon.

With graduation two weeks away, the Footprints staff decided to do whatever was necessary to grant her wish. They talked to social services about what would be needed to take

Figure 35 SSM Cardinal Glennon Children's Medical Center.

her out of the hospital. They worked with her physicians to be sure her pain and breathing were under control. They secured a portable ventilator, and one of our nurses, who took special training on how to use it, volunteered to go with her. Physical therapists worked with the patient several times a day so she would be strong enough to sit upright. They contacted the school to make sure her wheelchair could be on the graduation stage. Since she didn't want to go to graduation in an ambulance, they paid for a special van that would accommodate an electric wheelchair and a ventilator. Despite all of the preparation, on the morning of graduation, no one thought the young woman would be strong enough to attend graduation.

But she rallied. She was able to get up. She had her hair and nails done. She was dressed in a cap and gown. She talked to TV people as though there was nothing wrong with her. The staff helped her into the wheelchair and into the van. She arrived at her high school to massive cheers from her classmates. The 10 o'clock news that night showed her going across that stage to receive her diploma. She stayed out for three more hours before she returned to the hospital.

Not long after that, it became apparent that she was dying. Within moments of the young woman's last breath, her mother turned to Mary Ann Collins, director of Footprints, and Sister Judy Carron, the care coordinator, nurse, and chaplain. The grieving mother said, "You have no idea how important it was to her to graduate with her class. It's because you worked so hard that she was able to do it."

This is one of the many ways in which the remarkable people at SSM Health Care reveal the healing presence of God day in and day out, among our patients and among themselves.

8

Baldrige One More Time

For our fourth attempt at the Baldrige Award, we brought in Paula Friedman from our SSM St. Louis office to head up our efforts. The systemwide focus that Paula provided to our application in 2002 proved critical. So did her energy. If Paula slept from the time she came to the corporate office in January 2002 until the day in November when we learned we would receive the award, she did a good job of concealing it. Paula is a whirlwind of focused energy.

What did we do differently in 2002? We were very careful to link every one of our results to a core process identified in categories one through six. In other words, we connected the dots. We became intensely focused on our core customers—patients—versus assorted stakeholders. And we did a better job of explaining that we understood why we had achieved the results. In addition, we were able to demonstrate cycles of refinement rather than just improvements within processes. All of this gave a better sense that we would be able to sustain our improvements.

We were pleased when we learned that we would get a site visit in 2002. One of my favorite memories about that site visit concerns Bill Schoenhard, our system executive vice president and COO. In October 2002, we were preparing my closing remarks to the examiners. They had spent four days visiting hospitals across the system, and my closing remarks at

Figure 36   Paula Friedman.

the corporate office were our last opportunity to impress them. We'd worked hard on the remarks, and I felt we were ready. But Bill came into my office about 20 minutes before we were scheduled to meet with the examiners for the last time. Characteristically somewhat mild-mannered, Bill was impassioned. "Your remarks are not strong enough," he practically shouted. "They have to be stronger. You have to say that we are the organization that deserves to be the first in health care to receive this award!"

I can't decide if I was more shocked by his passion or by his comments. Frantically, I worked with our communications team to strengthen the remarks. Bill's passion was contagious, and strong words flew onto the paper like magic. Within minutes, the remarks were ready. They were strong, confident. I was ready.

Just as we printed out the final version of the speech, Bill stood in the doorway. He was having second thoughts. "Do you think we should ask someone else about what I just said?" he asked. "Absolutely not," we replied in sync, still charged up from his earlier comments.

Figure 37   Bill Schoenhard.

With my speech still warm from the printer, I walked into the room and faced the examiners and representatives from all over our system. As I delivered the remarks, I could feel my face flush with excitement. The speech lasted only six minutes, and I ended it with this:

> We've applied to Baldrige four times . . . always as a system. Along the way, people have suggested that we have just one of our hospitals apply instead of the whole system. There are some who say that a system can never win the Baldrige, that systems are too large and too complex.
>
> We believe that a system not only *can* earn the Baldrige, but that the system that *does* will make a lasting contribution to the quality of care in this nation. *We* are that system!
>
> Because we are living proof that other systems can push themselves to step out of their comfort zones to achieve exceptional results with CQI and the Baldrige Criteria. And the more systems that commit themselves to quality

improvement, the greater our ability to deliver health care breathtakingly better than it's ever been done before.

In closing, I'm reminded of a poem by the English poet Christopher Logue. To paraphrase:

> "Come to the edge," he said.
> They said, "We are afraid."
> "Come to the edge," he said.
> They came.
> He pushed them . . . and they flew.

You pushed us, and we flew.

THE CALL FROM THE SECRETARY OF COMMERCE

At 8 a.m. on November 19, 2002, I got the call from Donald Evans, then U.S. secretary of commerce, that we had been selected to receive the Baldrige. We later learned that although there were several health care applicants, we were the sole health care recipient that year. I allowed myself the luxury of spending the rest of the day ecstatic. Paula Friedman didn't believe me when I told her. Then she cried. All across the system, the excitement was palpable; people were genuinely thrilled that we had come so far and had achieved something so monumental.

It wasn't until the next morning that I forced myself back to reality. As the first health care recipient of the Baldrige, we knew that the eyes of the world would be on us, and the pressure to achieve exceptional results would be greater than ever. It had taken more than 24,000 employees, 5000 physicians, and 5000 volunteers to bring us to this level of quality.

A THANK-YOU

During the examiners' site visit to our St. Anthony Hospital in Oklahoma City, the examiners asked an employee in human resources what I should say to the president of the United States

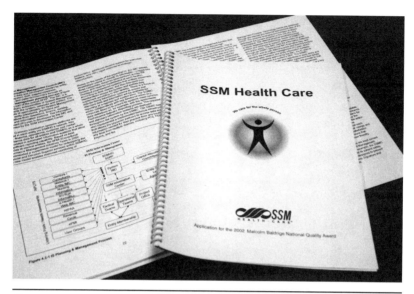

Figure 38 One of our Baldrige applications.

At 8 a.m. on November 19, 2002, I got the call from Donald Evans, then U.S. secretary of commerce, that we had been selected to receive the Baldrige. We later learned that although there were several health care applicants, we were the sole health care recipient that year.

---

if we won the Baldrige. She responded quickly, "Sister should tell him, 'Great things come from great people.'"

Not only did I say those very words when I accepted the award, but we produced an ad thanking employees for everything they did to help SSM Health Care win the Baldrige. The ad ran in every one of our communities.

A STORY

As I said, we were pleased when we learned that we would get a site visit in 2002. Earlier, I mentioned Sandy Lamer. Up until 2001, Sandy managed quality improvement at our Maryville, Missouri, hospital—St. Francis—and taught quality improvement classes all across our system. Sandy was

Figure 39   "Great things come from great people" ad.

one of the most positive people I've ever met—and an ardent champion of CQI and our Baldrige efforts. She was full of life, she had time for everyone, and, despite working in north-west Missouri, she retained the most pronounced New England accent I've ever heard.

In fall 2001, Sandy was diagnosed with a brain tumor. She underwent surgery, and subsequently radiation and chemotherapy. But the tumor was found to be incurable, and Sandy retired from her job to spend time with her family.

When I was in Maryville in early 2002 before we applied, I visited Sandy at her home. She was stretched out on a couch, weak from her radiation treatment, but she remained optimistic. She spoke of wanting to travel and see things she'd never seen before. Her spirit amazed me then, and it continues to amaze me every time I think of her. When it was time for me to leave, I bent to give her a hug. She looked at me and said, "Do me a favor?" "Anything I can do, I will," I told her. "Win the Baldrige this year, would you, Sister?" she said.

When I received word on November 19, 2002, that we had indeed won the Baldrige, Sandy was one of the first people I thought of, and I sent her flowers. Sandy died on February 22, 2003, just three months before we accepted the award. I mention this story not to be depressing, but rather because Sandy played such a significant role in our improvement efforts from our early implementation of CQI right through our applications to Baldrige. It seems only fitting to tell this story to honor her memory.

9

The Ceremony

Six months later, on May 21, 2003, the official ceremony was held outside Washington, DC. On the stage with me were the vice president of the United States, the U.S. secretary of commerce, Sister Jacqueline Motzel (president of the Franciscan Sisters of Mary), and the other 2002 Baldrige recipients. When it was my turn to speak, I talked about the commitment of our founding sisters, their determination to care for people who could not pay for their care, and how we continue that commitment today. I talked about how, as the first health care recipient of the Baldrige Award, SSM Health Care was living proof that health care in the United States was capable of improving, despite many predictions to the contrary. I said we were proof that health care organizations could push themselves out of their comfort zones to achieve exceptional results.

When I finished, I was greeted with thunderous applause. The entire audience rose, for the only standing ovation that day. I was perplexed. Only later did I learn that during my remarks the lights had gone out, leaving much of the room in darkness. People were amazed that I had never faltered. The truth is that the podium light remained on, and, frankly, I was so nervous I never noticed that the other lights had failed.

The turbulence that had characterized our journey to date would not leave me alone even for three minutes.

Figure 40 Sister Mary Jean accepts the Baldrige Award from Vice President Dick Cheney.

10

Learning from Baldrige

Our four Baldrige applications yielded more than 200 pages of feedback. Among our surprises was that the examiners essentially started from scratch with each application. Each year we received feedback from an entirely different group of people who knew nothing about us before they read that year's application. They didn't look at our past applications; they didn't even know whether we had applied before. All they saw was that year's 50-page application. Then, if they made a site visit, they could ask questions about anything in those 50 pages.

What was so surprising was how remarkably consistent the feedback was. That consistency certainly validated the process and, for us, the credibility of the findings from year to year. When nearly 30 different examiners visit you over three years, and each group each year says the same things, you start to believe that they know what they're talking about.

In four years of feedback, Baldrige repeatedly cited four strengths:

1. Our strategic, financial, and human resources planning process

2. Our ability to demonstrate commitment to our vision, mission, and values

3. Our use of CQI

4. Our focus on the patient

THREE KEY MESSAGES

Although we learned many things specific to our organization during our four applications, there were three universal messages. First, measure what you say is important. Second, compare your organization to the best, not just to the average. Third, have a process to consistently deploy strategic communications throughout the organization.

When we first applied for the Baldrige, our deployment process for important systemwide initiatives was inconsistent at best. I remember asking one of our senior executives if a certain systemwide message had been communicated to all the employees at one of our facilities. He assured me that it had been. I asked him how he knew, and he told me, "I just know." When I probed, he said, "I'm sure the message was communicated, because they're all good people at that hospital." Unfortunately, it takes more than good people; it takes good processes to ensure deployment.

HOW DO YOU KNOW YOU'RE GOOD?

Doug Ries is president of our SSM Cardinal Glennon Children's Medical Center, a wonderful place where the culture is steeped in compassion, caring, and doing whatever is necessary to minister to children and their families. Doug points out, "There is a palpable passion behind our care. We know we're good at what we do. But Baldrige asked us *how* we know. How do we demonstrate that we're good? Where is the measurement? Where is the rigor around accountability? It was like cold water in the face."

OPPORTUNITIES FOR IMPROVEMENT

Over the years, Baldrige feedback alerted us to many other opportunities for improvement, ranging from managing com-

Figure 41   Doug Ries.

plaints to integrating human resources—so essential in health care—into our strategic and financial planning processes. Our first application did not include human resources as part of our strategic planning process. Strategic planning to us was all about positioning, growth, and finance. At the same time, we told Baldrige how important our employees were to our organization. Again, Baldrige asked the obvious: "If your employees are so important, why aren't they part of your strategic plan?" Clearly the two are inextricably linked: Without human resources, all the strategic planning in the world won't achieve a thing.

SHARING OUR STORY

Since we won the Baldrige, I've had the opportunity to share our story with many people. We share information with anyone who wants it—through Baldrige Sharing days, executive exchanges, hosting international visitors, and putting our full application on the Internet (www.ssmhc.com) so anyone, including our competitors, can read it.

I have spoken to thousands of people all over the United States and abroad. I've been to Canada, Japan, Thailand, the Philippines, Sweden, and Korea, and I plan to visit Argentina and Brazil in the fall of 2007. Groups from Korea, Japan, India, and Brazil, as well as the Asian Productivity Organization, which represents 16 Asian countries, have visited us to learn about our Baldrige experience. Because this subject is so important to me, I have had to overcome my own reluctance to speak in public. I often tell people that the two things I dislike most are traveling and public speaking, and now I find myself doing a lot of both. Fortunately, I am only one of many executives at SSM who spend time sharing what we have learned.

During my travels, I have observed that many people don't really understand what it takes to apply for the Baldrige Award. They have heard about the award, they think it would be great to win it, and often they want to know the name of the consultant who wrote our application. Yes, we worked with a consultant, but we wrote the application, and we did the work the application described ourselves. And there is no magic formula—it was our employees, physicians, and volunteers who earned the Baldrige. They did it the hard way—every day, no matter how tired or stressed they were, they did whatever was necessary to bring our mission to life.

I bring people back to reality when I make these presentations. CEOs tell me they are not quite ready to take the plunge and they are waiting to apply. I say, "You will never be ready. So, you might as well do it when you're not ready. What you learn from that very first application is going to be so significant, you simply will not believe it." No organization, whatever its size or business, can see everything that is happening inside its own walls. That's why the feedback is so valuable—it shows you what's in front of your nose, so close you can't see it.

The Baldrige application process offers so many benefits. By providing a broader understanding about how parts of the

> *CEOs tell me they are not quite ready to take the plunge and they are waiting to apply. I say, "You will never be ready. So, you might as well do it when you're not ready."*

organization work together and affect each other, it encourages a systematic approach to improvement. By providing unbiased feedback, it helps an organization focus on the things that will help it achieve its goals.

FRAMEWORK, FOCUS, DISCIPLINE

In other words, the Baldrige provides a framework, a focus, and discipline. Although our CQI culture was firmly established prior to Baldrige, our approach to improvement was scattered, so it didn't have the overall impact that it could have had. Today, our approach to improvement flows directly from our mission. And, best of all, we're not changing our focus every year, as we did in our early years as a system.

Sister Susan Scholl says it this way: "You have to keep your focus on the customer. It's too easy to get pulled into private agendas. Hospitals have traditionally created systems that work for them but are terribly disruptive to patients and families. Baldrige has taught us to keep our eye on the patient. That's why we're here."

"Constancy of purpose" is how W. Edwards Deming described long-term commitment. I am proud that SSM Health Care has remained constant in our commitment to exceptional health care for 17 years. Despite turbulence and frustrations on our journey, in a world of chaos and rapid change, our constancy of purpose is a source of stability to everyone in our organization.

This constancy of purpose has become entrenched in our culture. For every thousand employees at SSM Health Care, we now have one Baldrige or state quality award examiner. The training required to become an examiner is intense, and the work is demanding, but the payoff is great. Our SSM Baldrige examiners serve as an internal cadre of consultants who understand best practices across industry lines. They visit and evaluate role model companies across the United States, and they use this information to improve SSM. Their goal is to help every employee and every physician in our organization focus on improving everything they do—for our patients.

11

Beyond Baldrige

Now that we've won the Baldrige Award, the last thing we want to do at SSM Health Care is to become complacent. The award is about *continuous* improvement. In health care, that's especially important, because it is our moral duty—our sacred obligation—to do everything we can to get better and better at caring for our patients.

These improvements, in my opinion, are only going to come from within health care organizations. They're not going to be mandated by the government, at least not anytime soon. As *Washington Post* columnist David Broder wrote not long after we received the Baldrige: "The conceit of Washington is that big changes in important services must be mandated from the outside—by legislation or regulation. But increasingly it is clear that systemic change in vital human service functions, such as education and health care, are more likely to emerge from the search for internal improvements than from external mandates" (April 9, 2003, p. A21).

MANY CHALLENGES

Even so, improvement from within won't be easy. We remain a very large and complex organization, including some 20 hospitals, home care, nursing homes, clinics, rehab facilities, physicians offices, and a technology center—spread across four states. The kind of dramatic improvement that a single hospital or even a small health care system can achieve rapidly is very difficult for a large and lumbering system such as ours.

Moreover, health care has unique challenges. While the Ritz-Carlton, another Baldrige recipient, is known for its superlative service, guests at the Ritz pay for that service. In health care, we are committed to providing the highest quality care whether or not our patients can pay. Just as our early sisters lovingly referred to patients who could not pay as Our Dear Lord's, we care for all who come to us, a commitment made increasingly difficult as states and the federal government cut people from the Medicaid rolls and health insurance becomes more and more expensive.

THE SCANDAL OF OUR BROKEN HEALTH CARE SYSTEM

In a nation as rich as ours, it is a scandal that so many people are denied basic, preventive care that would keep them well. Many Americans today must choose between feeding their family and seeking medical care. They put off going to the doctor, and when they become very sick, they seek care in the emergency room, the most expensive place to get care. Every day, over and over, we see the human toll of our nation's broken health care system. Yet through it all, we are driven by our mission: "Through our exceptional health care services, we reveal the healing presence of God." In the tradition of our founding sisters, we are committed to not only caring for the people of our communities, but to changing an unjust system in which 47 million Americans lack health insurance.

While we continually advocate at the state and national levels for justice in health care, we must also do what we can to change from within. With a workforce of more than 24,000 employees who come from all educational levels, a variety of cultural backgrounds, and many different faith and non-faith traditions, we have an unparalleled opportunity to create the conditions for change. As a large employer, there are a number of ways we can provide opportunities for personal growth for people within SSM Health Care.

LEADERSHIP AT ALL LEVELS

For many years, I have believed that organizational transformation—true, deep, and lasting change—will occur only when we call forth the leadership that resides within every person in the organization. Creating an organization of leaders takes energy and long-term commitment, but the potential exists to achieve greatness.

I can trace the idea of employees as leaders to the day we realized we weren't as good as we could be. It wasn't that we were bad; it was that we weren't fulfilling our potential. To be great, we would have to tap into the very best that every employee had to offer.

I've described how CQI and Baldrige pushed us to be better and focused our improvement efforts. The piece I have not described is our attempt to foster leadership at all levels of our organization. The concept is countercultural. When I ask people to name the leaders in their organization, they generally mention the CEO, the COO, the CFO, and others at the executive level.

I don't deny that these individuals must be accountable for the overall success of the enterprise. Clearly these titles represent one aspect of leadership. But the leadership that builds an exceptional organization is not the CEO making one pivotal decision. It's the minute-by-minute, day-by-day actions of everyone in the organization seeking to improve everything they do.

For many years, I have believed that organizational transformation— true, deep, and lasting change—will only occur when we call forth the leadership that resides within every person in the organization.

So many aspects of leadership occur outside the realm of the executive leader. When an employee from housekeeping takes the time to sit with a frightened elderly patient, she is demonstrating leadership. When the person at the cafeteria cash register steps forward to comfort a tearful man, she is demonstrating leadership. When a nurse's aide apologizes to a family that had to wait, he is demonstrating leadership.

Real leadership is not about authority, control, or giving orders. It's not about titles or executive benefits. Leadership is about taking the initiative to do a job in a more efficient way or a better way, treating others with respect and compassion, and thinking of ways to be helpful. A leader is someone who is confident of her or his abilities and freely expresses that confidence—not in arrogance, but in humility.

OWNING THE WORK

Leaders assume responsibility for what happens in their area of work. They "own" their work and perform their job with integrity, as an expression of themselves, their creativity, and their commitment.

One year during my site visits to all our facilities, I spoke to employees. In my remarks, I told them this:

> You are an SSM Health Care leader because you have initiative, creativity, the courage of your convictions and integrity, *and* you want to make a difference.
>
> And you're not alone in wanting to make a difference. We all want to make a difference. The question is, are we doing everything we can to ensure that all of us can

make a difference for our patients and for one another? Are we tapping everyone's potential for leadership?

The truth is, you may not even be aware of the many talents you offer this ministry. Let me ask you, how many of you go home from your job and in effect become a CEO, COO, or CFO of a small corporation called a family? And in this family, you oversee a whole host of functions, including dietary, transportation, finance, medical emergencies, community relations—you name it, you're in charge of it. You provide in-service education on topics ranging from spelling, to appropriate behavior in school, how to get into college, how to change a tire, and how to make grandma's chocolate cake.

And, not only do you manage the day-to-day operations, you establish a vision for the future, set appropriate goals, and put in place strategies to achieve that future.

But then you return to work. And perhaps you're told what to do and how to do it. The leadership abilities that are so evident in your home environment aren't always utilized in your work environment. That just doesn't make sense. And I believe it's an unforgivable waste of talent and potential.

Wherever I presented this message, employees related to it. As I spoke, I would see heads nodding in understanding and agreement. Employees want to contribute to the organization. It is up to executive leaders to create a climate that fosters leadership. Employees must understand that they are respected members of the team, regardless of their title and salary. They must be encouraged to articulate their ideas and to carry them out, and they must be encouraged to take risks, even if those risks end in failure.

SSM UNIVERSITY

One of the ways in which we hope to develop the leadership potential that resides within all SSM employees is through our new SSM University. We introduced SSM University in 2005, after nearly a year of asking people at all levels of our organization what skills they needed to do their job better. Through a series of focus groups, SSM University determined the types of educational programs that would support and nurture people at all levels of the organization. It will develop programs to support leaders in executive positions, in supervisory positions, and in mid- and entry-level positions in every department from transport to dietary, from medical records to administrative council, from nursing to laundry.

Many organizations focus exclusively on the executive and manager levels and ignore everyone else. To me, that approach is shortsighted. In health care, entry-level employees spend more time with patients than anyone else. So why relegate key training in patient satisfaction and personal development to executives and supervisors? It makes infinite sense to develop the leadership of the employees who are closest to our patients, as well as those charged with strategic decision making.

SCHOOL AT WORK AND VOICE

One of the programs SSM University offers to entry-level employees is School at Work, an eight-month program that prepares participants to further their education. School at Work is new to SSM Health Care. It is similar to a program, VOICE, that was started several years ago by our SSM DePaul Health Center in Bridgeton, Missouri. VOICE (Vision of Individual Commitment to Excellence) is designed to provide special training for entry-level employees with limited education and opportunities in life.

Figure 42   An SSM University School at Work 2006 graduating class.

Employees begin the voluntary VOICE program on their first day of employment. Discussions focus on how to get started in a new job and how SSM's mission and values relate to delivering food trays, scrubbing floors, making beds, or whatever the job is.

After 30 days, participants return for a two-day, 16-hour training program that covers a wide range of topics, including anger management, stress management, getting along with bosses, grooming, coming to work on time, and fulfilling job responsibilities. Participants learn interview skills and how to write a resume. They learn how to set goals, something new to many participants whose lives may have been focused on surviving. They are encouraged to think about where they want to be in five years. Do they want to be doing the same job? Do they want to be in school, training to do something else? This kind of critical thinking opens employees to possibilities they never realized might exist for them. Employees also learn about our reimbursement program, which can help pay for tuition if they decide to go to school.

The VOICE program helps employees understand that when they push a gurney, deliver food, or clean a room, they may be the bright spot in a patient's day. This understanding translates to better patient care.

The program has had a significant effect on retention. Before 2002, the retention rate for first-year entry-level employees at DePaul was 35 percent. Since the introduction of VOICE, the retention rate is 80 percent.

A FAIR AND JUST CULTURE

Hand in hand with developing an organization of leaders is creating a fair and just culture. This is particularly difficult in health care, where hospitals have traditionally punished people who made mistakes. I know that from personal experience.

Many years ago, when I was young nurse, I made an error and overmedicated a patient. Fortunately, the patient suffered no ill effects. I noted the error on the patient's chart but did not report it to anyone. When the resident made rounds, he circled my note on the chart in red ink. I was called before the director of nursing services and reprimanded. What was the likelihood that I would admit a future error by writing it on a patient's chart? What was the likelihood that I would talk to the supervisor about how the error could have been prevented in the first place? Very low in both cases.

Certainly I made a mistake, and I should have been accountable for it. But when the emphasis is placed on blame, we miss a valuable opportunity to prevent future errors. When we emphasize error *prevention*, the focus is on correcting the process breakdowns that resulted in the error.

As I hope is the case at all health care organizations, the safety of our patients at SSM Health Care is our number-one concern. Our Safety Clinical Collaborative has made many process improvements that have yielded a safer environment at all our facilities. Along with our clinical work come our efforts to create a fair and just culture. To that end, not only do we encourage people to report their mistakes, we ask them to report mistakes that *almost* happened—that is, near misses.

A program at our SSM St. Joseph Hospital West in Lake Saint Louis, Missouri, *rewards* employees for reporting near misses. The hospital holds a monthly drawing for prizes to reward employees who turn in near-miss forms. Employees who report that they almost made a mistake become eligible for a reward. In the first year, more than 100 forms were turned in, and 45 of those led to process improvements. In the areas where process improvements were implemented on the basis of the near-miss forms, the hospital has had zero errors. Following the program's success, we asked our other entities to adopt a reward system for near-miss reporting.

> *Not only do we encourage people to report their mistakes, we ask them to report mistakes that almost happened—that is, near misses.*

My role as CEO is to push people to achieve their potential. Every year when I visit our facilities, I talk with employees and examine the goals written on department posters and passports. If a department goal states, "We will give 95 percent of patients pain medication before they are in pain," I ask, "What about the other 5 percent of the patients? Is it okay that they're in pain?" Employees understand immediately that our goal should be 100 percent.

GOING TOBACCO-FREE

One of my efforts to push was not greeted warmly by about a fifth of our employees. In February 2004, I announced we would go tobacco-free—inside and *out*—the following November during the Great American Smokeout. I was tired of walking through walls of cigarette smoke whenever I entered one of our hospitals or seeing smoking huts that just happened to be under the name of the hospital. The final straw was when I was asked if we could heat one of the huts during the winter. I decided that as a health care provider, we would ban smoking on our campuses as a matter of integrity.

Once we had made the announcement, we had to figure out how to make it happen. We put together a Tobacco Free steering team, with representatives from most of our entities. The large group divided into eight subteams: Behavioral Health, Patients/Families/Visitors, Smokers, Physicians, Education, Security/Plant, Human Resources, and Communications. Over the course of about nine months, guided by the steering team, the subteams, and teams at all of our entities, we put together the support, communications, and policies that would be necessary for success. Despite the fact that roughly 20 percent of our employees were smokers, and they weren't happy, we moved forward. We showcased the smoking-cessation success stories of employees in our system newspaper, *Network*. I am especially pleased that Bill Odman, a co-chair of our Smokers subteam, has been tobacco-free for more than two years now, and there are many others who have given up smoking along with him.

Employees were fearful that patients and their families would rebel. Our SSM Cardinal Glennon Children's Medical Center was especially worried about the parents of children. Having a loved one in the hospital is always stressful, but when it's your child, it's particularly stressful. I understood that. But I felt that our role as a promoter of health in our communities called us to take an unpopular stand. We knew such a significant cultural change would take time, and we also knew that we didn't want confrontations with patients or families. So we told everyone to take a deep breath and do the best they could. If visitors persisted in smoking, we would remind them of our policy, but we would stop short of a confrontation. We provided smoking-cessation classes and plenty of advance notice to our communities, including letters to firms in close proximity to our buildings in case there was a problem with cigarette butts. Despite everyone's worst fear that going tobacco-free on November 18, 2004, would bring about the end of the world as we knew it, it was a non-event.

Since becoming tobacco-free as a system, we have received calls from more than 60 organizations asking for our advice about how to do it. We willingly share both our mistakes and our successes.

HEALTHY LIVING

Our success with the tobacco ban prompted us to launch our Healthy Living initiative in 2005. The initiative is still young, but it is SSM Health Care's commitment, over the long term, to foster environments that promote good health for employees, patients, and families. It goes back to the concept of change from within—of doing what we can to advance health. Healthy Living will mean healthy food in our cafeterias and vending machines; increased awareness about the importance of walking and exercising, with hallways and stairwells made more attractive to potential walkers; and health-risk assessments available to all employees. There will be tips for stress reduction, since health care is such a stressful field.

ACHIEVING EXCEPTIONAL PATIENT CARE

By far the largest initiative we've undertaken since 2002 is Achieving Exceptional Patient Care (AEPC), which began to take shape in early 2005. AEPC is designed to improve satisfaction throughout the system. At the heart of it are our five values: compassion, respect, excellence, stewardship, and community.

Figure 43 Materials for the Achieving Exceptional Patient Care Meeting in a Box.

The concept is simple: All of us must demonstrate our five values in everything we do—in our every interaction with patients, with families, and among ourselves. It is one thing to ask people to demonstrate our values in the work they do; it is quite another to be sure they understand the very specific ways that they can show compassion, respect, stewardship, excellence, and community in the work they do every day.

As with nearly everything we do, AEPC was designed by SSM employees for use by SSM employees. Teams from across the system, with a good mix of managers and nonmanagers, focused on eight elements: exceptional service standards, exceptional conversations, exceptional rounding, exceptional recognition, exceptional patient experiences, selecting exceptional employees, exceptional service recovery, and exceptional ideas.

As the teams worked to develop educational materials for each of the eight elements, a corporate office team focused on producing easy-to-understand materials (including a Meeting in a Box) that would convey the overall message. At the same time, we appointed AEPC champions at every entity, and periodically we convened the teams and the champions to ensure that we were on the right track. The candor of these meetings is one of the reasons the materials have been well received. We constantly sought to simplify the message so that already-busy employees could quickly absorb what they needed to do.

> *If a nurse takes time up front to greet the patient, introduce herself, explain what is going to happen, ask if there are any questions, and thank the patient, time will be saved later on.*

We emphasized that AEPC would provide the tools to ultimately make work easier. If a nurse takes time up front to greet the patient, introduce herself, explain what is going to happen, ask if there are any questions, and thank the patient, time will be saved later on.

Our goal with AEPC is to reach the ninety-ninth percentile for patient satisfaction as a system by 2007. It is a lofty goal, but one that is attainable.

Our SSM St. Joseph Hospital of Kirkwood, Missouri, has made remarkable strides since implementing AEPC. The emergency department has repeatedly scored in the ninety-ninth percentile for patient satisfaction, and several other departments in the hospital are very close. According to Sherry Hausmann, president, the achievement is the result of intense focus on results and rewards for achieving those results. In Sherry's words,

> Our administrative council has emphasized how important our results are, especially with the clinical directors. Our chief nurse exec talks about satisfaction scores while he makes his daily rounds. As a result, the clinical directors are focused on the data. All members of administrative council talk about our results during rounding.

We have recognized incremental steps and department progress by personally delivering small rewards (balloons, food, etc.) as a group. We have engraved a cup, and we fill it with snacks and deliver it to any department that achieves the ninety-ninth percentile in their particular portion of the survey.

When the emergency department achieved the ninety-ninth percentile, we very publicly acknowledged the achievement housewide, along with celebrations such as a barbeque and chair massages. As a result of this focused approach, we've shifted our culture to one where every employee knows how much we value patient satisfaction.

The culture in our ED is incredibly special. When we asked employees in the department in December 2005 what recognition they would like, rather than something for themselves they requested that we buy a dinner for them to personally deliver to the family of a sick child at the Ronald McDonald house. That culture of caring is what is driving our results.

Figure 44 Sherry Hausmann.

A MATTER OF INTEGRITY

From the very beginning of our journey to the present, our efforts have always been driven by something I find sorely lacking in the business world today: integrity. Recently we were asked to talk about the return on investment for our work to achieve excellence. We told the reporter that ROI has never been our motivation. Rather, we are motivated by our desire to provide the very best possible care for the people we serve. That, after all, is our mission.

In today's world, many people don't understand this approach to business. In a world where the dollar is almighty and corporate greed seems to run unchecked, now is the time to examine what we value. For several years, I've been hanging on to an article from *Fast Company* magazine because it predicts something I'd really like to see happen. It talks about the business community from a values perspective, and it describes "a profound transformation in business . . . a transformation in which the barracudas, sharks, and piranhas will disappear . . . and in their place will be *nice, smart* people with a passion for what they do" (Tim Sanders, *Fast Company,* January 2002, p. 64).

Our organizations are filled with nice, smart people with a passion for what they do. As people of integrity, we must tap their potential.

12

In Conclusion . . .

At SSM Health Care, the Baldrige helped us better understand the meaning of integrity. When Baldrige asked us, "What do you mean by 'exceptional'?" and "Why are you content to compare yourselves to organizations that are average?" one of the reasons I was so distraught was that in my mind, they had questioned our integrity. If we weren't willing to compare ourselves to and imitate organizations that are the very best—either in health care or in other industries—then our organizational sincerity—our integrity—was suspect.

"Integrity" means an organization must be what it says it is. If we say we provide exceptional care, then we must never cease in our efforts to improve. It's as simple as that.

Often, the greatest wisdom is simply put. Over the years, I've enjoyed saving various sayings, poems, and bits of wisdom that inspire me. From time to time I find hidden away a piece of paper with one of these bits of inspiration. The other day I found one that very simply sums up our efforts at SSM Health Care over the last two decades:

Press on. Nothing in the world can take the place of persistence. Talent will not; nothing is more common than unsuccessful men [and women] with talent. Genius will not; unrewarded genius is almost a proverb. Education alone will not; the world is full of educated derelicts. Persistence and determination alone are omnipotent.

—Calvin Coolidge

In the end, it is persistence that has kept us going—the sheer grit to hang on to the belief that we could become exceptional. I urge you—whatever your organization, whatever your role—to bear that in mind. SSM Health Care is far better than it was when we began, but we still have miles to go to be truly exceptional. We will persevere for two reasons: It's who we are, and it's the right thing to do.

For my part, I am grateful beyond measure for the amazing people I have met along the way, for the incredible work that has been done to bring SSM Health Care closer to exceptional, and for the privilege of being part of a healing ministry with a mission that constantly inspires awe: Through our exceptional health care services, we reveal the healing presence of God.

Index

Note: Page numbers in *italics* indicate figures.

A

Achieving Exceptional Patient Care (AEPC) initiative, 114

B

Baldrige Award, 2. *See also* continuous quality improvement (CQI)
application process for, 52–54
creating open culture for, 48–49
dry-run application for, 49–51
effect of, for SSM Health Care, 117–118
feedback from, 95–97
health care organizations and, 45
key messages of, 96
sharing story of, with other organizations, 97–99
SSM Health Care's first attempt for, 67–72
SSM Health Care's second attempt for, 72–75
SSM Health Care's third attempt for, 72–75
SSM Health Care's fourth attempt for, 85–90
Barney, Steve, 15, *16*
Berger, Mother Mary Odilia, 3–6, *3, 4,* 56
Brand, Kathy, 48

C

Calcaterra, Mary, 43, *43*
Cheney, Dick, 93, *94*
Clinical Collaboratives, 40–42
clinical results, measuring exceptional, 71
continuous quality improvement (CQI), 22–23. *See also* Baldrige Award
curriculum for, 27–29
"no bad apples" concept and, 32
physicians and, 39–40
positive experiences in implementing, 35
problems in implementing, 35–38
processes and, 30–32
resistance to change and, 38–39
Seven-Step Model of, 35, *36*
at SSM Health Care, 25
teams and, 33–35
Coolidge, Calvin, 118
CQI. *See* continuous quality improvement (CQI)
culture, fair and just, 108–109

D

Deming, W. Edwards, 6, 24, 99
department posters, 78, *78*
diversity, 15–17

E

exceptional clinical results,
      measuring, 71
exceptional health care services,
      defining, 69–72

F

Farren, Suzy, 58, *58*
Ferrigni, Fil, *41,* 41–42
Florida Power & Light, 34
Footprints™ program, 82–84
Franciscan Sisters of Mary, 7, 10–11
Friedman, Paula, 85, *86,* 88
Funches, Barb, *29*

G

God, revealing healing presence of,
      82–84
Greenleaf, Robert K., 20–21

H

Hausmann, Sherry, 113–114, *114*
healing presence of God, revealing,
      82–84
health care
      applying manufacturing principles
         to, 24–25
      exceptional, defining, 69–72
      improving complex process of,
         22–23
      justice in, 102–103
Healthy Living initiative, 111
hospitals. *See* specific hospital under
      SSM

I

inclusive language, 14–15
integrity, 115
intrapreneurship, 19–20

J

James, Brent, 23
Jelle, Laura, 73, *73*

K

Kosseff, Andy, 39–40, *40*
Krings, Jim, 30, *30*

L

Lamer, Sandy, 29–30, 89–91
Langston, Tom, 82, *82*
leadership, personal improvement
      and, 103–104
Levy, Ron, 15, 51–52, *52,* 65–66,
      66, 68

M

Meeting in a Box, *80,* 80–82,
      112–113, *112*
Miller, Rita, 47–48
mission statement, 51–52, 55–64
      "deep conversation" for,
         57–58
      development process, 56–57
      getting to essence of, 59
      presentation of, to SSM Health
         Care's board, 59–60
      rollout of, 60–63
Mother Odilia. *See* Berger, Mother
      Mary Odilia

N

"no bad apples" concept, 32
nonviolent language, 14

O

Odman, Bill, 110
Our Dear Lord's (ODL), 5, *5,* 102
"owning the work," personal
      improvement and, 104–105

P

passport program, 68, *69,* 77
personal improvement
      leadership and, 103–104
      "owning the work" and, 104–105
      School at Work program, 106

SSM University, 106–107
VOICE program, 106–108
physicians, CQI and, 39–40
Pinchot, Gifford, III, 19–20
Plsek, Paul, 28, 35
posters, department, 78, *78*
processes, CQI and, 30–32

Q

quality award programs, state,
46–48
quality management. *See* Baldrige
Award; continuous quality
improvement (CQI)
Quality Resource Center (QRC), 29

R

recycling, 13–14
Ries, Doug, 96, *97*
Ritz-Carlton, 102
Ryan, Mary Jean, *20, 24,* 65–66, *66*
acceptance of Baldrige Award by,
93, *94*
early life of, 7–9

S

Safety Clinical Collaborative,
108–109
Schoenhard, Bill, 13, 85–86, *87*
Scholl, Susan, *42,* 42–43, 99
School at Work, 106, *107*
Showcase for Sharing, 48–49
SSM Cardinal Glennon Children's
Medical Center (St. Louis,
MO), 82, *83,* 96, 110
SSM Health Care
AEPC initiative at, 111–114
becoming tobacco-free at,
109–111
creation of, 11–13
development process for mission
statement of, 55–59
diversity at, 15–17
early history of, 1, 3–7
effect of Baldrige Award for,
117–118
first attempt for Baldrige Award
by, 67–72
future challenges for, 101–102
Healthy Living initiative, 111
leadership conferences at, 19–22
nonviolent/inclusive language at,
14–15
opportunities for personal
improvement at, 103–115
presenting mission statement to
board of, 59–60
recycling at, 13–14
rollout of mission statement for,
60–64
second attempt for Baldrige Award
by, 72
starting CQI at, 25
tapping potential within, 22–23
third attempt for Baldrige Award
by, 72–75
SSM St. Joseph Hospital (Kirkwood,
MO), 30, 113
SSM St. Joseph Health Center (St.
Charles, MO), 31
SSM St. Joseph Hospital West (Lake
St. Louis, MO), 31, *32,* 109
SSM St. Mary's Health Center (St.
Louis, MO), 37
SSM University, 106–107, *107*
St. Anthony Hospital (Oklahoma City,
OK), 89, *90*
state quality award programs, 46–48
St. Clare Hospital (Baraboo, WI),
33, 73
St. Francis Hospital & Health
Services (Maryville, MO),
29–30, 46, *47,* 77
St. Mary's Hospital (Madison, WI),
8, 48–49

T

teams, CQI and, 32–35
30-30 guarantee, 31–32

Thompson, Bill, *11,* 11–12, 21, 22, 35

Tisdel, Yvonne, 15, *16*

total quality management (TQM). *See* continuous quality improvement (CQI)

V

VOICE (Vision of Individual Commitment to Excellence) program, 106–108

Vrabec, Peter, *33,* 33–34

W

Widmer, Lynn, 37, *38*